UNIVERSITY
OF NORTH CAROLINA
STUDIES IN
COMPARATIVE
LITERATURE

NUMBER 44

UNIVERSITY OF NORTH CAROLINA
STUDIES IN COMPARATIVE LITERATURE

Founded by Werner P. Friederich

Editorial Committee

William J. DeSua, Editor

8. Nan C. Carpenter. RABELAIS AND MUSIC. 1954. Pp. xiii, 149. Paper, $ 1.75. Cloth, $ 2.25.
17. A. Levin. THE LEGACY OF PHILARÈTE CHASLES. Vol. I. 1957. Pp. xxviii, 248. Paper, $ 6.50.
20. James W. Hassell, Jr. SOURCES AND ANALOGUES OF THE NOUVELLES RECRÉATIONS ET JOYEUX DEVIS OF BONAVENTURE DES PÉRIERS. Vol. I. 1957. Pp. 208. Paper, $ 4.00.
32. William J. DeSua. DANTE INTO ENGLISH. A study of the Translation of the Divine Comedy in Britain and America. 1964. Pp. xii, 138. Paper, $ 3.50.
33. Francisco López Estrada and John Esten Keller, Collaborators. ANTONIO DE VILLE-GAS' EL ABENCERRAJE. Introduction, Original Text and Translation. 1964. Pp. 86. Paper, $ 2.50.
35. Eugene F. Timpe. AMERICAN LITERATURE IN GERMANY, 1861-1872. 1964. Pp. 95. Paper, $ 3.00.
36. Frederic Will. FLUMEN HISTORICUM: VICTOR COUSIN'S AESTHETIC AND ITS SOURCES. 1965. Pp. ix, 97. Paper, $ 3.00.
37. Helmut A. Hatzfeld. A CRITICAL BIBLIOGRAPHY OF NEW STYLISTICS APPLIED TO THE ROMANCE LITERATURES, 1953-1965. 1966. Pp. 184. Paper, $ 7.00.
38. Jules Gelernt. WORLD OF MANY LOVES: THE HEPTAMERON OF MARGUE-RITE DE NAVARRE. 1966. Pp. x, 170. Paper, $ 5.50.
39. Lawrence Marsden Price. THE RECEPTION OF UNITED STATES LITERATURE IN GERMANY. 1966. Pp. 246. Cloth, $ 6.00.
40. Werner P. Friederich. AUSTRALIA IN WESTERN IMAGINATIVE PROSE WRITINGS, 1600-1960. Pp. xv, 280. Cloth, $ 7.50.
41. John Philip Couch. GEORGE ELIOT IN FRANCE: A FRENCH APPRAISAL OF GEORGE ELIOT'S WRITINGS, 1858-1960. Pp. vii, 197. Cloth, $ 6.50.
42. W. LaMarr Kopp. GERMAN LITERATURE IN THE UNITED STATES. Anglo-German and American-German Crosscurrents, Vol. III. Pp xx, 230. Cloth, $ 7.50
43. James I. Wimsatt. CHAUCER AND THE FRENCH LOVE POETS: THE LITERARY BACKGROUND OF THE BOOK OF THE DUCHESS. Pp. ix, 186. Cloth, $ 6.50.
44. Yvonne Rodax. THE REAL AND THE IDEAL IN THE NOVELLA OF ITALY, FRANCE AND ENGLAND. Four Centuries of Change in the Boccaccian Tale. Pp. ix, 138. Cloth, $ 5.50.

For Reprints from this Series see page 137

Foreign Sales through Librairie E. Droz, 11 Rue Massot, Geneva, Switzerland.

THE REAL
AND THE IDEAL
IN THE NOVELLA

OF

ITALY, FRANCE AND ENGLAND

FOUR CENTURIES OF CHANGE
IN THE BOCCACCIAN TALE

by

YVONNE RODAX

C. W. Post College of Long Island University

CHAPEL HILL

THE UNIVERSITY OF NORTH CAROLINA PRESS

1968

Printed in the Netherlands by Royal VanGorcum Ltd., Assen

FOR GRETEL

FOREWORD

The world of Chaucer is considered first in this study because the criteria of comparison are qualitative and the beginning of the changes in the novella which are traced throughout the following chapters can be clearly seen in Boccaccio.

To all of those generous mentors at New York University whose inspiration and help have borne fruit in this work, the author is most grateful: to Dr. Robert J. Clements for his gift of the whole world of comparative literature and the particular territory of the novella, as well as for the direction of this book; to Dr. John Atherton and Dr. Anna Balakian for valuable constructive suggestions; to Dr. Richard Harrier for his careful reading and comments; and to Dr. John H. Fisher and Dr. Francisco Ayala who have also been generous with their time and thought. To Dr. Maurice Valency of Columbia who first opened the magic gates of the realm explored here, the author owes a particular tribute. And to Dean Eugene Cantelupe of C. W. Post College go special thanks for his help in finally bringing the book into the material world.

Y.R.

CONTENTS

CHAPTER ONE

INTRODUCTION

All of the world's best tales convey to the reader a vivid sense of reality, but the sources of this vigor range between two extremes. The realist, who sees the world as a physical entity lying outside of himself, experienced by the senses and mapped by the intellect, recreates it in words as exactly as he can.[1] The idealist, looking within, mirrors the truth which he discovers within the brightly colored realm of his own psyche. The unification of these disparate views constitutes the task of the writer and the challenge of human existence.

The major literary artists of all time (including the best of the novellieri) have all worked a kind of white magic with the world. By evoking a counterfeit presentment of her essence and her shape, each one has helped to preserve a vision of wholeness, sustaining her fundamental duality while gallantly concealing it almost as well as she does herself. Even Boccaccio in the *Decameron*, with tongue in cheek, makes such courteous concessions that her integrity suffers no outward damage; by those who wish to see, she may still be seen in his tales to possess both a body and a soul. Much later, a Wordsworth or a Rilke can each feel, in a personal way, that he is engaged in *creating* that soul by spiritualizing the matter which is presented to him in experience, but it was Plato,

[1] This process, however, can never *duplicate* reality, as Frye points out: "One could hardly find a more elementary critical principle than the fact that the events of a literary fiction are not real but hypothetical events. For some reason it has never been consistently understood that the ideas of literature are not real propositions but verbal formulas which imitate real propositions." Northrop Frye, *Anatomy of Criticism : Four Essays* (Princeton, 1957), pp. 84-85.

I

ages before them all, who set the standards for idealists to come by means of his ladder and firelit cave.

The earliest forbears of the tale took shape in the realm of myth and song—a process which is still repeating itself endlessly in the realms of childhood and of primitive man. Out of the ancient literary substratum the quality now called realism gradually appeared.[2] Since the essential power of any myth tends to evaporate with repetition, all such narratives gradually become dessicated and prosaic, or acquire new vigor by assuming dramatic form.[3]

The most powerful chants of primitive man do not spring from the pressure of physical needs or the joy of satisfaction. (In the former case he is much too occupied for song, and in the latter, too replete.) They are voiced in a blind effort to create a realm—or to communicate with such a place—in which the puny strength of man is given another dimension through the interest of powers both benign and terrible.[4]

Poets and mystics of all ages have succeeded in convincing many of their fellows of the reality of a supernatural order which impinges at every point upon the realm of the senses, but which is accessible only to those who will submit to its transcendent and mysterious laws. Deity, muse and oracle—as well as demon, ghost and incubus—all bear witness to a mighty psychic power which has been coursing through the body of mankind for untold centuries. This force, lying beyond human good and evil, nevertheless demands respect in terms of a stern moral dichotomy. The prophet and oracle make clear to man his duties and his transgressions as well as the supernatural importance of his destiny. The poet, *éntheos*, may also use his moments of vision to sing of higher

[2] Stith Thompson has demonstrated this process admirably by analyzing the manner in which the Finnish teller of folk tales, Vinokurova, has retold the "meager, unified...self-sufficient" folk materials of her race and showing that she tends to individualize the characters, play down the supernatural and heighten the dramatic impact. The realistic detail which she supplies from her own experience is especially noteworthy. Stith Thompson, *The Folktale* (New York, 1946), p. 453.

[3] Ibid., p. 460.

[4] Joseph Wood Krutch, in his discussion of tragedy, has noted the psychological truth that "under certain conditions desire produces belief"—and has taken the stand that "this ability to will a belief may bestow an enormous vital advantage" upon the believer. Joseph Wood Krutch, *The Modern Temper* (New York, 1956), pp. 95-96.

2

things, but more often moves subtly down the scale to transform the ordinary world of nature and of man.[5]

All poetry and mythology springing from the souls of interpreters who are convinced that they are channels of communication between two worlds fills an enormously important function; it forms strong, invisible bonds uniting the mind and heart of man. With the gradual separation between thought and feeling beginning in the seventeenth century these ties became fewer; Descartes, having with the best of intellectual intentions slit the throat of poetry, died in happy ignorance of the gash which this act inflicted on the psyche of modern man. In our own time Yeats and the *Symbolistes* have pulled together the sides of the wound almost by main force and Eliot, ironic minstrel of the split and paralyzed soul, finally transcended his poetic function to find a unity beyond the realm of art—and hence, to some critics, betrayed his aesthetic trust. A fusion of categories is not permissible in an age which has lost sight of the whole.

In that strangely compelling new realm between art and science which has been explored by Freud and Jung there has been found a partial explanation for the illness of modern man and a hint of the means by which his sundered parts may be reunited. Jung, whose synthesizing gift is akin to that of the artist, has led many individual human beings back through the tunnels of their own psyches to that wildly beautiful kingdom known to the poets of all ages and all times. Here the dragons and the princesses, the fatal trees and mystic serpents all exist in *actuality*—for "the archetype does not proceed from physical facts, but describes how the psyche experiences the physical fact."[6] This ancient land, at once the most familiar and the least explored of territories, has been proved once more in our own time to be a reality far more vital to man than the world of sense. The dream-world has been shown by scholars

[5] " 'Poetry is religion which is no longer believed.' " Krutch borrows Santayana's "famous phrase" in his discussion of this subject. Krutch, p. 97.

However, this crucial idea goes back to Boccaccio's day; he sets it forth in his *Vita di Dante*: "Theology is a 'poem of God,' a poetic fiction." Francesco De Sanctis, *History of Italian Literature*, trans. Joan Redfern (New York, 1931), I, 303.

[6] Carl Gustav Jung, *Collected Works*, ed. Herbert Reed, Michael Fordham, Gerhard Adler (New York, 1953), IX, 154, 156.

to be so closely related to the land of faërie and myth that there is no doubt as to their original identity. It makes little difference whether Mephistopheles is a real fiend from a real hell or an "archetype" which may be described as an aspect of Faust's personality "capable of dramatic projection"[7]—he smells of real sulphur all the same. Marlowe, unbeliever and former divinity student, who knows him better than does Goethe, shows the Fiend dragging off the scoffer's soul to a place with which every psychiatrist is professionally acquainted.[8]

Interpreters of the realm of the supernatural have been known by many names. Prophets, magicians, priestesses, a few fortunate apostles and apparently accidental or chemical illuminates—all, from Tiresias down to Aldous Huxley under mescalin—not to mention a whole army of poets—have borne witness to a region in which the senses as we know them do not operate, but which is almost invariably described in language glittering with sensuous imagery, often of the most realistic kind. The intellect need not sleep while the poet writes, but if it is well disciplined it will yield precedence to the Muse. Pascal, surprised with an ineffable vision, was powerless, for all his genius, to translate it into words, since apocalypses do not lend themselves to terms compatible with conic sections and computers. Light, color, pattern—live and meaningful— and mystic harmony characterize the happy visions of that other world, and the nightmare glimpses of disorder, frustration and agony which are the other side of the coin derive their very horror from the absence of those graces and benisons. The symbolic exchange of palette and plume which spiritually linked painter and poet through the Renaissance and into the seventeenth century acknowledges a kinship extending far beyond the words, the sounds or the colors through which it is expressed.

Life for the idealist is surpassingly rich, but by no means dependable— and this state of affairs is reflected in the world which he depicts. Events do not move in a reasonable sequence for Basile's Cenerentola any more than they do for Chaucer's Griselda or Bandello's lady in the lions' den.[9]

---

[7] Frye succinctly phrases this aspect of Jung's theory. Frye, p. 291.

[8] Goethe's Mephistopheles is no archetype, but a literary caricature designed with romantic confidence to demonstrate the *impotence* of the archetype; hence he fails to capture Faust, becomes enamored of the equally impotent angels and is reduced to a laughing-stock.

[9] Bandello's point of view in this tale is borrowed.

4

Things customarily turn into their opposites, and if the creator of such a world is in love—either with his God or with an idealized lady—he may dwell in a state of exquisite antinomy, as did Petrarch in the stylized landscape of the troubadours and St. John of the Cross, blinded in the glory of his Dark Night. This is about as much equilibrium as can be expected in a region whose climate and topography are mirrors of the soul.

Not the least of the demands which this region makes upon the idealist is that of distinguishing good and evil[10]—not by rule, but at first hand. In his highest state he is preoccupied with the discovery of mysterious laws which he must both interpret and obey. Further down the scale, in the world of the novella, the problem is most often one of conflicting choices, or of recognizing the better of two alternatives. Boccaccio's King Pietro refuses a young girl's love on one plane in order to perpetuate it on another; the "litel clergeon" of Chaucer's miracle must choose between his primer and celestial song; the muleteer's wife of the *Heptameron*, struggling for her life, finally chooses death. In each case, the actions or qualities of the character serve to make manifest in the world of fact an intangible verity, and are intended to serve as a model or an inspiration for lesser folk.

The realist, on the other hand, expresses a truth demonstrable by practical experience and reason. A mind like that of Freud is impelled to describe the domain of the mystics in terms of a super-neurosis[11] and to stake out under the term *Id* that abyss which to Conrad appears as an impenetrable Heart of Darkness. There is little room in this mapping process for the indeterminate and the ambiguous. The work of the realistic writer, in the form of facts, pseudo-facts or histories, reflects the physical plane; anecdotes must at least purport to be taken from life. Among the novellieri included in this study, Des Périers, Marguerite of Navarre and Bandello steadfastly hold to the premise that everything which they describe actually happened; they all take pains to supply

---

[10] Wilbur C. Cross, *The Development of the English Novel* (New York, 1899), p. 187. Cross stresses the "direct or implied moral purpose" of the idealist, and calls him "a conservative defending the ways of Providence."
[11] Sigmund Freud, *The Future of an Illusion*, trans. W. D. Robson-Scott (New York, 1949).

concrete data which, although it may not be authentic, always appears to be.

Humor for the realistic writer is derived from a limited double vision which on its lowest level produces the sadistic practical joke, usually at the expense of the gullible or innocent. Des Périers' collection, particularly, abounds in thick-witted peasants who take things literally—always fair game for the trickster. Beyond this there are progressive levels of merriment ascending through the fabliau realm (inhabited largely by cuckolds, and common to all the novelle) to the heights of sparkling wit displayed in Boccaccio's tale of Ser Ciappelletto and Chaucer's vignettes of the Monk, the Friar and the Pardoner. At this level there appears the world's best satire, with all its lancets ranged against social suppuration. An ironic detachment pervades the finest literature of this kind;[12] when it breaks down, the mood becomes savage and cynical, as in Fenton's occasional attempts at satire in the *Tragical Tales*.

The realist is attracted to the use of two very different kinds of literary style. His concern for form may lead him to create verbal structures which, like those of Pettie, become more intricate in a direct ratio to the weakness of his abstractions, or he may discard artistic canon altogether and strive for plain language in the interest of verisimilitude. Bandello professes to take the latter course, and when he holds to it he achieves some noteworthy effects. However, he often departs from it in order to clothe a passage or a whole novella in fashionable rhetoric. Such a writer, sensing at times that he must make a stronger connection with real life, will often attempt to enliven his material with dramatization and sensationalism in the manner of Boaistuau and Belleforest—but to no avail. The increasing separation between the outer and inner worlds, brought about by the pressures of a materialistic society, robs him exactly as it robs the idealist. Neither of these dual aspects of human nature can function creatively for very long without relationship to the other; each has its indispensable kind of richness, which dwindles in isolation.

The Italian novella of the Renaissance, precisely because it is a spontaneous, rapidly-spreading popular form, presents a rich field for the

[12] Frye notes that "wit detaches the reader; the oracle absorbs him" and that "irony is consistent...with complete realism of content...." Frye, pp. 276, 277, 224.

study of man's concept of his world during a period of far-reaching change and stress; its imitators (and Chaucer, in his own right) demonstrate variations of that idea, colored by individual and national temperaments as well as by changing times. Here we may observe in a conveniently small scope the changes which occur within the ideal world as a corollary of those taking place in the realm of fact. Among the writers to be discussed there are a few whose works grow richer with every reading. Even the mediocre novellieri, however, help to reveal to modern man, as in a crystal ball, an image of his changing world.

CHAPTER TWO

THE WORLDS OF THE CANTERBURY TALES

By the time that Chaucer decided to make good use of the ancient treasure-trove available in his day to the teller of tales, Boccaccio had already been before him and had designed for his own collection an intricately worked literary casket into which he placed not only a generous quantity of antique pieces, but also a number of cunning facsimiles. These, since they look almost exactly like originals, are not easy to detect; nevertheless, the gay skeptics of his own time were fully aware that some of his coins impudently distinguished themselves by displaying a smiling face on either side.

It seems unlikely that the English poet knew the *Decameron*,[1] although his own coffer, like those of the myriad imitators of *Giovanni della Tranquilitate*, bears a family resemblance to it. However, the one great difference between the *Canterbury Tales* and Boccaccio's work stems from the fact that English literary craftsmen of the fourteenth century were laggard in some matters as compared with the Italians, and had not yet learned the art of moral ambiguity. All of the contents of Chaucer's casket may be taken at face value; nothing appears to be what it is not. Hence we must bring his collection into our counting-house first in order to know how to evaluate the contents of the rest, including

[1] Mario Praz, *The Flaming Heart* (Garden City, 1958), pp. 74-78. Also H. C. Cummings, *The Indebtedness of Chaucer's Works to the Italian Works of Boccaccio* (Menasha, Wisconsin, 1916), pp. 176-180, 195-196. (This Princeton dissertion was also published in 1918 as part of the *University of Cincinnati Studies*, 2nd Ser., x, Part 3.)

the *Decameron*, which became a model for all collections to follow.

To one who looks closely, it becomes obvious at once that in addition to a few experiments formulated from old designs and minted by himself, Chaucer has provided us with what in his time was an antique but remarkably comprehensive currency, and that it is with this *totality* that we must be concerned rather than with relative numbers, weights or denominations. The value of the collection lies as much in its completeness as in the soundness of its components—and with this treasure it is still possible, as it was in the author's own day, to purchase a world complete.

Since the time of the troubadours, the metrical narratives extant in Chaucer's day had been divided into two kinds: the ideal, filled with beauty and the real, flaunting its opposite. A poet like Cavalcanti might employ them both without causing confusion among his admirers, and Chaucer called both kinds "tales."[2] His admiration for Dante stopped far short of any attempt to imitate the synthesis of the *Commedia*, and he remained content to shadow forth in the *Canterbury Tales* that "double world of Gothic art and thought"[3] which enclosed the separate facets of human existence. There is no hint of relative values in his collection, but nothing is left out.

As we examine the separate coins, one stands out among the group, not only because of its beauty but because it reveals a skilful synthesis of elements; the result is a richness rarely achieved in the novella form. For all its delicacy, it is remarkably solid; it also displays great artistry in design, and may well be designated as the finest individual piece in Chaucer's box. This is the *Prioress's Tale*, which not only beams with the serene and childlike faith characteristic of the miracles of the Virgin, but brings that tender glow down into the world of mundane affairs and spiritualizes the whole scene.

In the Prioress's invocation the poet sets to soft verbal music the transcendent themes of mother-love and innocence which, embodied

[2] This dichotomy is represented by the *novas* and the romances, although Chaucer cheerfully blurs the distinction. Wilbur Cross, *The Development of the English Novel* (New York, 1899), p. xiii.

[3] Wylie Sypher, *Four Stages of Renaissance Style* (Garden City, New York, 1955), p. 37.

in human characters, are soon to reappear within the tale itself. The transition to the earthly plane, however, is complete. There is no doubt that it is a real world in which the "litel clergeon" trudges back and forth each day. Although Chaucer has little space within his twenty-nine stanzas for description, he builds a foundation of salient details: the ghetto-street, with its sinister activities;[4] the crowded little school "doun at the ferther ende"; the impending Christmas season; a statue of the Virgin, somewhere between the widow's home and the fatal street; the obliging older boy; a lesson-book; the seven-year-old child's bare knees.

The narrative, enlivened with touches of schoolboy dialogue, is infused midway with a sound of unearthly sweetness—the antiphon, sung in clear treble. This sound, which rings out twice a day above the sordid business of the street, actually constitutes the essence of the miracle; its dramatic fulfilment in death simply serves to manifest its source. Something ineffable, reaching gently down, has "perced" the heart of the child; love, returned spontaneously in the form of purest song, joins earth to heaven.

The thread of sound which forms this metaphysical connection is dynamic and powerful, releasing forces of evil as well as good. Here again it is the author's carefully selected detail which keeps the action on the earthly plane—the murderer's clutch, the gross reality of the "ward-robe" where the small body is thrown, the mother's sleepless night and desperate search. The slender singing throat is actually cut—to the "nekke boon"; burial, after the mass, is a practical matter, to be accomplished without delay; at the final revelation the abbot, overcome, falls "gruf" upon the ground, and the pavement is suddenly strewn with wonder-stricken monks.[5]

The fundamental law of nature has been suspended for all to see, but the "litel clergeon" remains a real child to the very end. At the crucial moment he needs the warmth and tenderness of a mother's love—and

---

[4] The reader is not expected to question the medieval convention which locates Satan's wasp-nest "in Jues herte."

[5] Chaucer's subtle humor, always manifest in his descriptions of the real world, is evident even at this solemn moment.

it will not fail him even though he leaves the real world behind. This, in its full emotional reality, is what enfolds him with the words,

> "My litel child, now wol I fecche thee...
> Be nat agast, I wol thee nat forsake."

The poet has skilfully preserved the simplicity of his source-tale (which exists in numerous analogues), while infusing it with music and life. The contemporary versions, however, portray an older child; many of them restore him comfortably to life. Chaucer selects and alters his detail to enhance a theme which is more profound than mere religious magic— the incalculable power of innocence, its heavy cost and ineffable reward.

The coin which seems at first glance to resemble this matchless piece most closely is actually very much thinner and lighter in weight. The *Second Nun's Tale*, although it contains the same kind of supernatural material, never makes the crucial connection with the real world. Valerian's vision and the angel bearing flowery crowns are mere scenic decorations in comparison with the little schoolboy's Virgin, who never appears to the reader at all. The fault does not lie with the celestial messengers, but in the fact that Chaucer has not been interested in putting Saint Cecilia into a world which is solid enough to offer contrast. There is some promise in the beginning, when Valerian stoutly asserts his manhood:

> "...And if thou love another man, for sothe,
> Right with this swerd thanne wol I sle yow bothe"

but it is not sustained. For all Chaucer's grace and fluency, this tale gives the impression of being told at third or fourth hand, and the miracles and martyrdom dwindle into pious abstractions.

The *Man of Law's Tale* is a coin of still lower denomination. The story of Constance is a kind of rambling and adventurous exemplum set off with some minor wonders, but the main emphasis is upon the rapidly shifting action. This allows the author little opportunity to use his subtler skills in developing and integrating real and supernatural elements.

There is another piece, however, of a different category altogether, which may be identified immediately as one of exceptional quality. Although it does not possess the radiance of the *Prioress's Tale*, it is noteworthy for its unification of different literary levels as well as for its vitality and humor. Chaucer's inspired idea of putting an ordinary beast-fable into a mock-heroic setting has turned the *Nun's Priest's Tale* into one of the richest and most skilfully turned of his whole collection. By adroitly switching back and forth from epic sublimity to the weeds and dust of the barnyard he runs the gamut of his many talents while refusing to take any of them too seriously; the effect is one of incomparable *sprezzatura*. Since the satire is not directed at society but simply at the romance form itself (which he controls superbly when he likes) and the venial flaws of doting husbands and wives (for whom he holds a genuine affection in spite of all that he knows about them) there is not a trace here of the coarse disillusionment and cruelty which mark most medieval satire. Even "daun Russell" is not actually villainous, but turns out to be rather childishly cooperative. "In feith, it shal be don," says he, opening his mouth and letting the protagonist escape—thereby proving that all those comparisons to Judas and Ganelon have been nothing but rhetoric. At the end, as each dupe turns his own stupidity into a moral precept, the fox actually vies with Chauntecleer in displaying a kind of disarming humility—vulpine, of course, but edifying.

The realism in this tale has two levels—that of the poultry-yard, which is expertly drawn, with meticulous detail, and the level of human psychology. Chauntecleer's relationships with Pertelote and the fox and his reactions to his own dreams are adroitly interwoven with the clucking, treading and wing-flapping which enliven the widow's little "yeerd." Still, this princely bird would not be the memorable character that he is if he were not also an ideal creature—the finest cock in all literature. He is distinguished not only by his plumage of burnished gold, his castellated coral comb, azure legs and bill of gleaming jet, but by his music and his mystic relation to the equinoctial circle, and hence to time itself. In this ideal state the bejewelled bird makes connection with the supernatural world; he receives prophetic dreams and merges into a romantic prince, just as the mundane lord of the henroost becomes a fatuous human husband. When the author calls down execrations upon the fox—"O newe Scariot, newe Genylon, / False dissymulour, o Greek Synon"—daun Russell is represented as the betrayer of nothing less than an *ideal*; hence no epithet is too extreme. The tone is very different from that of the passage in which Chauntecleer in the tree-top and the fox below engage like old cronies in a kind of sheepish bickering—for here they appear in their realistically humanized state. But when the fox is streaking off across the fields with his prey flung over his shoulder and the whole neighborhood whooping after him—the most dramatic scene of all—we are back again in the vivid realism of nature, from which all the other levels derive their life. This story, better than any other except the *Prioress's Tale*, displays the author's versatility and skill in moving between two worlds and in keeping them not only related but firmly and indissolubly unified.

In the tales of the Pardoner, the Friar and the Canon's Yeoman the action is used as an object-lesson to convey a moral truth, which Chaucer's realism helps to emphasize. In the "tale" of alchemy, however, technical descriptions threaten to run away with the story, which is salvaged at the end by the tardy moralizing of the Yeoman. In each story the reader finds himself in a vividly colored medieval scene, full of action and rascality. In the first two, the supernatural appears suddenly and with disarming simplicity in the midst of the natural world; it gives fair warning (which goes unheeded) and finally assumes control. There is no confusion as to values, no sympathy to be wasted on the evil-doers. In the third, the Yeoman, bleary-eyed, leaden-hued and oppressed with debts, has finally concluded after seven long years that the philosophers' stone can never be found, that trickery does not pay and that he himself is a dupe.

The religious ending appended to this enlightenment smacks more of the style of Geoffrey Chaucer than of this seedy character, who would surely have sung another tune if he had succeeded in filling his pockets. The tale thus narrowly escapes turning into a rather weak and plotless fabliau of the trickster-exposed variety, rendered credible by a wealth of alchemical lore. The sudden moralizing turn is unexpected, but is still sound enough to shift the whole rambling exposé into the exemplum category at the end. Nevertheless, there is something lacking here—that direct and personal experience of the supernatural which makes the strange encounters with the Old Man in the *Pardoner's Tale* and the Friar's ominously "gay yeman" under the "grene-wode shawe" so mysterious and compelling.

The *Monk's Tale*, which comes next in the accounting, appears to have been added for bulk. It turns out to be a bag stuffed to bursting with small pieces stamped with similar markings, but comprising two very different kinds. Some, dealing with righteous retribution, are frankly didactic; the others, which simply catalogue reversals brought about by blind Fortune, are merely gloomy. Of the whole group, very few[6] come to life. It is no wonder that in the midst of their copious clatter the usually courteous Knight cries out, "Namoore of this!"

So far, we have been dealing with stories in which (with the exception of the *Nun's Priest's Tale*) the ideal is represented by a supernatural good. We now come to a group in which this is replaced by sheer human virtue. As in the religious stories, the danger in this kind of narrative lies in its tendency to become thin and abstract when the ideal loses touch with life. However, Chaucer has retold the history of Griselda with so much tenderness and grace that her humanity shines through that obdurate patience which to modern eyes appears misguided if not actually psychotic. Since she is a medieval type of virtue, however, created in an age in which patience had a place and in which each ideal quality could be pushed without popular objection to its excruciating extreme, it is no small victory for Chaucer that his Griselda retains her personal hold on the reader from the time that she first sets down her water-pot to greet the "Markys" until she trudges slowly along the road from the palace "in hir smok, with heed and foot al bare."

Virginia, in the *Physician's Tale*, however, does not fare so well. Her dilemma is no less agonizing than Griselda's, and is enhanced by what might be some rousing erotic melodrama and bloodshed, but for all that, she never comes to life. We do not know, as we do in the case of Griselda, how she prepared her green vegetables, her preference in mattresses or the state of her everyday coiffure. Virginius' daughter also suf-

[6] These include *Cenobia* and *De Hugolino Comite de Pize.*

fers other slights and deprivations; she is kept speechless until the end of her life when, amid a few custom-made laments, she swoons; arising to make her one really touching speech—her plea that her father "with his swerd sholde smyte softe"—she finds the words snatched abruptly out of her mouth and put into indirect discourse. The result is that Virginia's virtue, like the fortitude of her parent and the Olympian dye of her hair, remains abstract. This coin, then, although it is stamped with a fine old classical imprint, is so thin as to be practically valueless today.

There is another sizable pile of pieces, however, which glitter as brightly but which respond with a richer clink and feel more solid in the hand. These are tales in which the ideal values can be seen to shift almost imperceptibly into another scale—that of chivalric romance. In the *Franklin's Tale*, the finest of these, the gleaming chastity of the Christian exempla and the durable old Roman virtue are poured into a soft matrix of courtly love—with outstanding success. The supernatural, which is a purely magical element in most of the Breton lays (which Chaucer seems to be imitating or partly following here)[7] is in this rendition allied with the moral powers of the universe; it forces Dorigen to face the issue squarely. Chaucer's charm and skill in shaping the tale of *amour courtois* infuse life into this problem of conflicting values; its solution is satisfactory to humanist, to courtly lover and Christian alike—and even though the main characters may all appear to become rather formidably noble, they are set in an unusual situation. Chaucer's perfect lovers are married; thus Dorigen is required to manipulate *two* courtly swains, and she satisfies both without offense to Church, state, or Andreas Capellanus—a remarkable achievement in any age.

At first glance the *Knight's Tale*, which closely resembles that of the Franklin in charm and atmosphere, appears to surpass it in richness. Certainly this valiant attempt to condense into 2250 lines all the terrestrial and Olympian panoply of the *Teseide* is impressive. However, aside from a short-lived conflict between friendship and love, in which both Palamon and Arcite go down before Venus with identical dispatch, there are no real issues. It is not only impossible to choose a genuine protagonist, but it is difficult to tell Emelye's suitors apart; hence she sensibly

[7] F. N. Robinson, *The Poetical Works of Chaucer* (Boston, 1933), p. 826.

remains neutral. Being "fressher than the May" she qualifies automatically as the prize of the tournament, and this is all that we need know of Emelye.

When Mars and Venus take sides, matters become a little more clear, if not more elevated; these deities operate with the perfunctory air of operatic supers, but they come in at the right time. The supernatural sphere exists in this tale as a literary convention; it lends a certain expansiveness to the plot and an air of epic dignity to an affair which is in reality a magnificent pageant, rich in color and verbal music, detailed as a fine tapestry and stylized to such a point that Chaucer often seems to be gently satirical:

> "Why woldestow be deed," thise wommen crye,
> "And haddest gold ynough, and Emelye?"

This matter-of-fact naiveté is even more effective when it is combined with a hint of the burlesque:

> Arcite is coold, ther Mars his soule gye!
> Now wol I speken forth of Emelye.
> Shrighte Emelye, and howleth Palamon...

Best of all is the ironic effect when the frenzied activity on earth disrupts supernatural arrangements:

> Mapul, thorn, bech, hasel, ew, whippeltree,—
> How they weren feld, shal nat be toold for me;
> Ne hou the goddes ronnen up and doun,
> Disherited of hire habitacioun...

Nevertheless, though the tale boasts no genuine spiritual nor emotional values and presents (except for a few vividly descriptive passages in the tournament) nothing remotely resembling reality, it remains a delightful monument. Athenians, Thebans, fictional monarchs of Thrace and "Inde"—all are English knights in fantastic guise—denizens of that ideal world of "trouthe and honour, fredom and courteisie" which in Chaucer's time was beginning to vanish like a dream.

The *Squire's Tale*, an exquisite fragment, is curious in that it seems to represent an attempt on the poet's part to mould a medallion of his own, with a composite design derived from numerous ancient coins—a project which he apparently relinquished when the task became too demanding. The supernatural here is sheer magic, and the moral element, for all the exotic trappings, is the same convention of "heigh reverence and obeisance" which sustains the *Knight's Tale*. The effect is tantalizing, and it is no wonder that Spenser was inspired to complete this delicately mysterious design.

The *Wife of Bath's Tale*, a coin which superficially resembles those of the Knight and the Clerk, and is, like them, imprinted with many an elegant antique device, has nevertheless a very different ring. There is obviously some difference in the quality of the metal. It is not so much the Arthurian design which sets it off from the two just described, but a subtle change in the convention. This hero, for all his courtly bearing, has neither virtue nor bravery. He begins his adventure with a rape, loses his reputation, forfeits his life, is rescued by sheer luck and fails to fulfil his honest bargain. Chaucer takes pains to reveal him finally, at the absolute nadir of the courtly ideal, as he "walweth" miserably in the bed of his ancient spouse. And how does this anti-knight conclude the affair? In character, of course—as a caitiff. He has become the thrall of Woman, who demonstrates with judicial clarity the inexorable facts about herself: false and fair in youth, true and "foul" in horrible old age. This story, which Gower worked into a neat exemplum on obedience and courtesy and which in the older versions is a fairy-tale involving the reader in no commitments whatsoever, turns in the mouth of the Wife of Bath into the harshest realism. This is by no means obvious, for the story itself constitutes a charming veil, but the reader is given fair warning at the very beginning, through the sly remark about the "lymytour":

> Wommen may now go saufly up and doun
> In every bussh or under every tree;
> There is noon oother incubus but he.

In spite of the traditional Celtic trappings, the gracefully ambiguous moral and the magical ending, the underlying point of this tale expresses the disillusion of the fabliau—and thus appears to be particularly appropriate to its teller.[8] Nevertheless, it remains in its own category, for the generous measure of realism hidden in this story detracts not a whit from its style and grace. In fact, it has a merrier tone than the *Knight's Tale*, and reflects none of the courtly pallor which, even in Chaucer's day, had begun to look a little affected.

Last in this category comes another fragment, but even in this state, a masterpiece. *Sir Thopas* is a remarkable production which Chaucer has achieved by combining all the designs of argent romance into one— and then turning it ludicrously upside down. If it is difficult to determine the true character of the "lusty bacheler" wedded to the ancient crone, there is no such problem concerning the chaste knight of the "sydes smale" and "semely nose," whose saffron beard and hair flow down to his middle—the knight who feasted upon licorice and gingerbread, "clamb" into his saddle and ambled off to meet a giant with three heads, who threatened all comers with a sling-shot. Harry Bailly, that literal fellow, listens through thirty-one jogging stanzas and can bear no more—but to Chaucer the Pilgrim, whose naiveté accommodates the truth on several levels, this is "the beste rym I kan!" It is indeed one of the most skilful parodies in the English language, and probably the funniest. Although no modern reader can catch all of the myriad allusions, it is obvious that only a poet capable of refashioning all of the popular romances—if only he had the time—could have so deftly epitomized them. The smile which was only a flicker in the *Knight's Tale* but which broadened into a sardonic grin most artfully concealed in the story told by the Wife of Bath here bursts into rollicking laughter. However, it is not the chivalric romance which Chaucer is mocking; that is a form which he loves with all his heart. It is simply the mediocre tales, outworn and lifeless, which he must laugh to scorn.

But even though the knight's fiery charger shows signs of thickening

---

[8] This subtle correspondence may not have been intentional on the author's part; he may have intended the story for someone else at first. Nevertheless, the appropriateness is noteworthy.

and slowing down to a dapple-gray "amblere" as the age of chivalry declines, there are some things which can be depended upon not to change—one of which is practical common sense, ageless, solid and satisfying. One may not become inebriated on a fable, but it sticks to the ribs. There is a kind of morality which stands at the intersection between the real and the ideal, and although only two of the *Canterbury Tales* exemplify it, one of these is the *Nun's Priest's Tale*, which we have already placed among Chaucer's finest stories. The other also concerns a bird—Phoebus' white crow, who could both sing and speak. He talked too much, was forthwith plucked, dyed black (the process, considering the lack of feathers, remains mysterious) and thrown out of the house—the devil take him! This is the essence of the *Manciple's Tale*, and the particular scandal which the bird reveals adds spice to the proceedings, but is no more essential than the fact that the deceived husband happens to be the Sun-God.

> My sone, ful ofte, for to muche speche
> Hath many a man been spilt, as clerkes teche.

Read Solomon, continues the story-teller, read the Psalms, Seneca—it is all the same good sense, call it what you will. No matter what you feed a bird, it will go after worms; any cat will forego milk and meat to chase a mouse. And in like manner,

> Flessh is no newefangel, with meschaunce
> That we ne konne in nothyng han plesaunce
> That sowneth into vertu any while.

This is not exactly religious teaching, nor is it purely secular. It is the kind of wry moral conclusion about mankind that has been repeated for centuries, and which fits in neatly wherever it is called for, like the more important precept concerning the wisdom of holding one's tongue. The whole thing has a kind of solidarity to it, but not much life—simply because Chaucer has not considered it necessary to do much here but moralize. It is a procedure which he obviously enjoys and which he knows that his contemporary readers will accept with good grace and perhaps even with relish. To Phoebus he has allotted empty histrionics and to his spouse the classical reticence to pursue her amorous inclinations offstage. Strangely enough, the crow emerges in his single speech as an exceedingly salty and sophisticated character:

> "By God!" quod he...
> "For al thy beautee and thy gentilesse
> For al thy song and al thy mynstralcye,
> For al thy waityng, blered is thyn ye
> With oon of litel reputacioun
> Noght worth to thee, as in comparisoun
> The montance of a gnat, so moote I thryve!"

This feathered mentor, like Pandarus, obviously embodies more than a little of Chaucer himself; hence the reader cannot help regretting Phoebus' undignified haste in plucking such a perceptive fowl and flinging him out of doors.

Now that we have taken account of two-thirds of the contents of our treasure-chest, there are only two coins left, except for a small pile in which all of the pieces boast such untrammeled frankness of design that they are obviously related. It is true that the attitudes of most of the figures are crude and lascivious, but no more so, in fact, than those of the gargoyles, demons and other grotesqueries adorning the medieval cathedrals—all of which, secure in their appointed niches in the cosmos, represent the antitheses of the angels and the saints. Without them the vast spiritual scale would be lacking in its lower register, and without the fabliaux Chaucer's universal currency would be incomplete. These pieces are limited in circulation to a grossly material realm in which intangible values, whether religious or chivalric, are absurd, and there is no time to waste on moralizing even at the level of the fable. The rule is every man for himself in the satisfaction of his appetites—and since this involves constant conflict, the admirable fellow is he who finally gets what he wants, by force or by duplicity. In this realm the weak, the innocent and the feeble of wit are all fair game; once the reader accepts this premise, a remarkably consistent value-system begins to emerge. This is not moral, but practical—balanced delicately and precisely upon a fulcrum of ironic firmness. Here, where man appears to be homogeneous in substance there are none of the frustrations imposed by the agonizing duality of body and soul. In the fabliau, folk always get exactly what is coming to them.

The finest and most lively examples invariably demonstrate this law of compensation, which functions like a moral code in that it preserves human existence from falling into chaos. A man or woman can learn how to get along by this rule and, if all the facts are available, can anticipate exact results. He who is poor must depend upon trickery, hypocrisy and deceit; he who is rich can satisfy his desires by force or purchase until he falls victim to one more clever or more powerful than he. Marriage is an evil which can be ameliorated in a number of ways and beauty, like money and virginity, obviously exists for the purpose of being seized. In this universe, as in the moral realm, there is a hierarchy of offenses which lead to ignominy, punishment or destruction. The greatest of these is to disobey or disregard the laws of unregenerate human nature. Culprits who have offended thus include the Carpenter in the *Miller's Tale*, January with his aphrodisiacs and all the other fatuous old husbands of blooming girls. So gross is their sin against all the joyous forces of life that formal morals appear illusory in the face of it. The merchant of Seint Denys in the *Shipman's Tale*, far more interested in "chaffare" than in wholesome connubial pastimes, suffers consequent loss in both departments. Absalom fails to act completely like a man; this would be a venial sin if it went no further than preening himself like a popinjay and chewing licorice "to smellen sweete." Unfortunately for Absalom, however, he is not only "squaymous" but silly; the punishment strikes suddenly and surely in his most vulnerable spot—his fastidiousness.

The next greatest sin is stupidity and its concomitant, pride. The Carpenter's lack of wit costs him a broken leg and his reputation as a sane citizen—light penalties for a capital offense. Symkyn of the *Reeve's Tale*, by nature sly as medieval millers come, has turned snobbish like his spouse, and with as little reason. The honor of his womenfolk, symbolic of property and prestige, is a comic obsession with him. Alayn and John, working out their private revenge, unwittingly act as instruments of that ironic law which extracts from scalawags as blind as the miller exact payment—and in kind. It is this retribution which gives exquisite balance to what would otherwise be merely a salacious anecdote. No one but Symkyn suffers any ill effects from the nocturnal confusions; everyone else, in fact, is quietly gratified—and if Malyne sheds a few tears, they do not fall for her vanished maidenhood, but for Alayn.

Hende Nicholas, who knows the old game backwards and forwards, appears to be the perfect protagonist for a fabliau—and so he would be if Chaucer had not combined two separate plots in the *Miller's Tale*. Nicholas must perforce become a victim after his triumph over the Carpenter, but the author is too fine a craftsman to let this occur by chance. What happens to this fortunate lover is an object-lesson on foolish pride. Nicholas becomes too cocky over Absalom's discomfiture, loses his head and tries the same trick again. For this enormity he pays with a considerable expanse of seared flesh, for the rule of the fabliau is inexorable: *Do unto others or be done by.*

In the far simpler tale told by the Summoner, the Friar renders no spiritual sustenance to the ailing Thomas, but only insult—first, by way of his wife ("... And hire embraceth in his armes narwe/ And kiste hire sweete, and chirketh as a sparwe") and second, through a superfluity of windy talk. There is no offense to fabliau convention in either of these procedures, but the Frair, intoxicated with the sound of his own preaching, is guilty of pride. For this blind spot he is rewarded with precisely what he gave—an insult which indelicately but neatly takes the form of wind.[9]

It is interesting to note that those characters in the fabliaux who manage to go scot-free—Alison, "fresshe May" and Damyan in the pear-tree, Alayn and John, and the merchant's wife of Seint Denys and daun John

---

[9] It is probable that Chaucer never intellectualized the neatness of the retribution; his remarkable balance is usually more a matter of creative intuition than of wit. As for the anticlimax concerning the division of Thomas's gift, it is merely an extension of the insult to the whole opprobrious race of friars.

the friar—are neither exceptionally clever nor possessed of evil intent. They are usually young, lusty, shameless and uninhibited—Nature's favorites, forsooth. (They are also Chaucer's—and, in consequence, the reader's.) That ambiguous lady "Proserpyne" who comes to the aid of May dressed up like a fairy queen and chattering anachronistically of "Salomon"—who is she but Nature herself, stubbornly intent upon her own designs? It is she who supplies the answer which satisfies blind morality and leaves the way open for further ingenious variations in the game of outwitting a dotard. Although Chaucer has adorned this tale with a mélange of allusions and solemn debates which lend a literary tone, it remains in essence the acrobatic old pear-tree story, outrageous as ever, and played out with scant apology in full view of the audience:

> Ladyes, I prey yow that ye be nat wrooth;
> I kan not glose, I am a rude man—

The Parson's sermon and the *Tale of Melibee*, to modern taste, do not really belong with the rest of Chaucer's treasure; hence it is difficult to express their value in current literary terms. From one point of view the religious discourse is sheer idealism—pure "whete" as contrasted with the "draff" of most of the other tales; from another, it is a masterpiece of realism—an authentic sermon which still might be delivered to the faithful in small sections, providing that they could keep awake. However, it is lacking in the music and imagery which set up spiritual reverberations; the reader or listener is expected to get in tune as best he can by means of his intellect, his own faith and the whisperings of conscience.

In an age when the Seven Deadly Sins possessed as morbid a fascination for the popular mind as psychoanalysis does today, Chaucer's Parson would always find an audience—especially among pilgrims. Besides, his contribution abounds in earthy illustrations which for unabashed realism make the fabliaux seem innocent and gay. Human peccadillos are far from merry in the Parson's world, because the perpetrators know exactly what they are doing. So does the Parson. When he evokes glimpses of long robes trailing through the dung, abortion by drugs and by means more terrible, the "fool lookynge" and "vileyns touchynge" which lead to wantonness—even when he presents the more ludicrous aspects of masculine anatomy revealed in parti-colored hose—he is describing a real world in which *superbia, invidia, luxuria* and all the rest are not products of the churchman's mind but of living flesh.

The *Tale of Melibee*, however, because of Harry Bailly's impatience with the Pilgrim Chaucer's "dogerel," might seem at first glance to be chosen with malice aforethought. Here is *prose* with a vengeance, deliberately sententious and allegorical. Nevertheless, it is a familiar and popular form—a "moral tale vertuous," the avowed purpose of which is not to entertain but to edify. Once the reader puts himself in a receptive mood, he can find a certain medieval pleasure in searching out the correspondences—the names, symbolic wounds, the old conflict with the world, the flesh and the devil—nor will other rewards be lacking if he persists. The didactic framework is so earnest, dry and matter-of-fact that the proverbs and aphorisms with which it is studded sometimes take on an almost inebriating richness of flavor, from sheer contrast. The moths in the fleece and the "smale wormes" in the tree, the whole race of women vanquishing their husbands by "wikked conseil," the "litel thorn" that may "prikke a kyng ful soore," the unfortunate wight who, having gobbled his honey, must spew it up again, and that frail wench Fortune, apparently attired in gilded porcelain, who appears so clear and shining but is "the more brotil and the sonner broken" for all that—all these lend just enough sensuous imagery (at second or third hand) to keep the whole discourse from degenerating into a moral crossword puzzle. Still, Chaucer's contemporaries, hungry for tales to a degree which we cannot begin to appreciate, and also for quotations, for allegories, apothegms, anecdotes, allusions and practically anything *moralisé* —hungry, in fact, for words in almost any form—could feast with some satisfaction even upon such fare as *The Tale of Melibee*. It is Chaucer himself who, by "emancipating" his verse[10] (but not his prose) from the chains of medieval allegory, has given us a taste for his exceptional blend of vitality, humor and grace, and who has made us, with regard to the mediocre literature of his time, very difficult to please.

[10] Sir Walter Raleigh, *The English Novel* (London, 1894), pp. 6, 7.

Since the *General Prologue* contains much material which has been tracked down by researchers and made to jibe with historic fact, it is deceptively easy to think of it all as realistic. There is the Tabard, a real inn, and the pilgrims, complete with warts, beards and vital statistics, and there is of course the Wife of Bath, exuding reality with every breath. Nevertheless, one scholar has demonstrated persuasively that the pilgrims are always anchored firmly within the inn, even when traveling. This "bilocational, bifocal and bitemporal effect,"[11] if it exists, should certainly lend a giddy surrealism to the excursion. However, Chaucer's narration is done in retrospect, not on the spot; hence he has a perfect right to shift his point of view, which he does with considerable fluidity, but never to excess. The only actual strain on the verisimilitude of the frame is the fact that the characters are not equipped with microphones so that their companions can hear the stories over the clop-clopping of the hoofs.[12] Actually, Chaucer can be shown to be a more practical and thoroughgoing literary realist than is the figure conceived as industriously describing real knights, ships and beaver hats. He quietly sees to it that the reader is clearly (and almost always, completely) informed about the salient aspects of the pilgrimage, and accomplishes his purpose through the use of innumerable details, carefully selected to create an illusion of reality. The most literal reporter can do no more. Once Chaucer's characters begin to draw breath and get into motion, he leaves them to their own devices—an eminently practical and realistic procedure. There is no evidence that he ever became neurotic or threatened to call off the excursion because of a minor difficulty such as the impossibility of counting heads or the ambiguous state of that "unworthy sone of Eve," the Second Nun.

This is the charming and unfettered realism beloved by the medieval creative mind—that meticulous abandon which could allow the illuminator of a Book of Hours to take incredible pains in reproducing every fold in a saint's garment, every wave in the Red Sea—and then to fill the sky with golden flowers. Chaucer often appears remarkably modern

[11] Ralph Baldwin, *The Unity of the Canterbury Tales* (Copenhagen, 1955), p. 57.
[12] Kemp Malone, *Chapters on Chaucer* (Baltimore, 1950), p. 195. Professor Malone has pointed out the auditory complications of the pilgrimage.

in his intermittent periods of fidelity to the external world, but we have no reason to believe that *he* felt any such commitment.[13] Along with such solid fellows as the Miller, the Shipman, the Franklin and the Doctor, there rides a Knight who has rust-spots on his tunic—and incorporates sheer perfection. The Prioress who keeps her fingers out of the sauce also manages quietly to radiate the beauty of all the heroines of romance. The Parson, all but an Apostle reincarnated, nevertheless boasts a "Southren" origin and a brother who pitches dung. No one could appear more single-minded and earthy than the Wife of Bath; why is it not in the least disturbing to discover that she is learned, rhetorical, allusive and logical beyond belief? Would Harry Bailly actually speak rudely to the Franklin,[14] take the part of a bedraggled Yeoman against the Canon, cut off a pilgrim (and customer) contemptuously in the midst of his tale, or shout obscenities at the Pardoner—no matter how he felt? Factual answers to many such questions might reveal a pattern of small anomalies running like the crackle in a glaze over the entire surface of the Tales—but the illusion of real life created in the Prologue remains whole and undisturbed.

Chaucer has accomplished this by working in two directions: *outward*, from the abstract concept or prototype represented by each personage, and *inward*, from the material world in which he has securely anchored each one as individual. It is here that we find a wealth of wonderfully pertinent detail—the furred wrist, the green and coral rosary, the sweat, the cropped head, spindle-shanks, drunken bellow and absent-minded stare. The convergence of these separate lines of literary approach results in a *Prologue* which is bursting with life—but which seems to be completely lacking in that rich and mysterious vein which shines intermittently throughout the tales. The presence of the Parson is certainly insufficient to supply it. As Chaucer has painted him, he lacks body, and thus cannot communicate spiritual vitality to the reader. Nevertheless, there is something invisible and elusive which permeates every character and

---

[13] Chaucer was "not deeply concerned with plausibility or verisimilitude either in plot or in characterization." Malone, p. 197.

[14] Malone, pp. 186-197. The initial question above, raised in Professor Malone's discussion of the Host, gave rise to the rest.

links the whole motley procession with earth and heaven too. It is not allegory, for turning Canterbury into a symbolic Jerusalem—for all but a mystic like Blake—would congeal the blood in every rider's veins. This is a miniature *society* on pilgrimage, not a set of personified qualities or sins—but the amalgam which welds it together is spiritual, even in the face of that society's manifest duality and inconsistency. It is the tacit but living faith of the poet himself—the salient quality of the age in which he lives and which he is portraying here—which can "knytte up al this feeste." It acts as an invisible catalyst for the exposure of the corrupt and supports the weak, the mediocre, the greedy and the shifty-eyed within a framework based upon free will as well as upon clearly defined moral law. Within this structure not even the Pardoner can remain completely sterile. His outrageous impudence and avarice, the physical repulsiveness of his state—all are negative aspects of humanity, used dramatically to set off the bluff masculinity of the Host, the Parson's humility, the aristocratic generosity of the Knight and the delicate lily-fragrance evoked by the invocations of the Nuns.[15] Since the Pardoner's presence can never counterbalance such wholesome realities, he arouses in his fellow-pilgrims neither horror, astonishment nor lasting contempt; no more serious censure comes his way than a kind of official rebuke (which actually serves to restore his fellowship with the group) and a good deal of sane and refreshing laughter.

That vision which renders the imperfections of this world *comic* rather than tragic depends primarily upon a feeling of security.[16] This is ordinarily gained through religion, art, sheer intellect or some combination of these, but the common denominator is that salutary detachment which comes with finding a vantage-ground outside the human condition. Religion offers another dimension in the supernatural realm; art imparts to life a principle of aesthetic order, and intellect puts the sorry

[15] This is of course not the only literary use to which the author puts this unsavory character; he is an instrument of satire and a kind of grotesque decoration, ornamental in reverse; and there is still, in the medieval view, as much hope for him as for any of his fellows if he takes care not to die unrepentant.
[16] Horace M. Kallen, "The Aesthetic Principle in Comedy," *American Journal of Psychology*, XXII, p. 37, summarized, in Ralph Piddington, *The Psychology of Laughter* (New York, 1963), pp. 204-205.

scheme of things into a system or renders it ridiculous through wit. Chaucer has access to all three of these means of detachment, and makes full use of them. For this reason his humor is exceptionally rich, varied and sustained. Gifted with the wit to comprehend the complex ironies of human existence and the skill to give them point, rhythm and brilliance, he is a supreme master of the comic; but there is an even greater resource lying behind all of this—the faith which renders his laughter warm, spontaneous and tolerant. That merriment is unlike any which has been heard since. Even the gloomy note of the *Retractation* cannot completely drown it out, but simply helps the reader to understand it better.

The double vision which reveals things not only as they are but as they ought to be finds its own means of expression—irony, exaggeration, parody—in all of which Chaucer is highly skilled; its highest expression would be satire if he had no resources beyond his wit. However, he is a true poet, modestly making light of the celestial afflatus for the most part, but allowing it to flow into musical and pictorial patterns which are still as "fresshe as May," for all the pains which he has expended upon them.

When he falls into prose, this artist, at least so far as the modern reader is concerned, loses both his style and his identity—but such an idea has never occurred to him. When he speaks, through the Parson, of the heavenly Jerusalem, he is didactic and dull—but convinced. It is the reflection from those streets of gold which infuses his finest tales, subtly irradiates all his colors and warms the lifeblood of his men and women; it is the music from that realm which regulates his own poetic pulse. For one of so broad and so simple a vision, nothing in life is small or commonplace, and nothing is impossible. In April woodlands the "smale foweles maken melodye" and so, in the sordid tavern, do the "harpes, lutes and gyternes"; Nicholas strumming his "gay sautrie," the "syngynge" Squire and chanting Prioress, Chauntecleer of the swelling throat, "murier than the murie orgon," the miraculous "litel child" with the Virgin's pearl beneath his birdlike tongue and the "aungels of God" bearing garlands, white and red—all must be forever taking wings in song.

28

CHAPTER THREE

THE WORLDS OF THE DECAMERON

Giovanni Boccaccio, like Chaucer, was many men in one—a complex human being who succeeded in unifying his personal realm by means of the poet's heart hidden beneath the various exteriors which he presented to the world. And, like Chaucer, he presented in his collection of tales an extraordinarily detailed and vivid replica of that world, drawn partly from experience, partly from the rich mine of popular literature, and partly from the wellspring of genius, that mysterious source which makes a few human beings in every age the spokesmen of their time. The English poet, younger by a quarter of a century, brought forth in his own country the picture of an age already vanished in the land of Dante and Boccaccio—an age best represented by the medieval procession.[1] This is an allegory of human life, with a common starting-point, an orderly progress and a dependable destination. The myriad squabbles, ironies and disturbances to be observed upon this route can no more affect the majestic course of the pilgrimage than a zephyr can alter the pathway of the stars. Chaucer's *Canterbury Tales* are not allegorical in intent; nevertheless they reflect in their very structure and universality this characteristically medieval concept of life.

Boccaccio's artistic problem was much more difficult; a procession of human lives in the politely skeptical Trecento could do little more than appear out of a vacuum at one end and vanish into a gulf at the other—a structural impossibility; but they could be contained by other means. It

[1] Northrop Frye, *Anatomy of Criticism: Four Essays* (Princeton, 1957), pp. 52-53.

was not for nothing that Boccaccio was born with an artist's soul—analytic, intuitive and perfectionistic all at once, and in love with the stately intricacies of classical rhetoric as well as the delights of a sensuous imagination. Reality, crumbling away with the vitiation of religious faith, could be restored by preserving it within an aesthetic framework, a process which was as useful to literati as to the painters of the Renaissance, as Frye has pointed out. However, the life which is seen inside these "picture-frames" has been completely divorced from the medieval vision; the ultimate reality is now no longer "moral, religious or naturalistic" but aesthetic.[2]

And so the old medieval duality, which seems to be the only really workable concept which has so far been hit upon in man's attempts to explain his own nature, has for Boccaccio completely disappeared. However, within his framework of architectural periods and verbal arabesques he proceeds as briskly and optimistically to paint a picture of human life as if he were not fencing it in out of chaos. His method is so ingenious and so subtle that it is well worth closer examination.

After a courteous bow in the direction of the ladies and some sentimental chit-chat concerning personal obligations (which sounds more moral than it actually is) he begins the discourse of the First Day with a sudden access of verbal power:

Questo orrido cominciamento vi fia non altramenti che a' camminanti una montagna aspra ed erta, appresso alla quale un bellissimo piano e dilettevole sia riposto, il quale tanto più viene loro piacevole quanto maggiore è stata de salire e dello smontare la gravezza.

Here, obviously is a viewpoint based on something serious and real, beginning with the unspeakable horror of the plague, but promising peace and comfort at the end. *"E sì come la estremità della allegrezza il dolore occupa, così le miserie da sopravegnente letizia sono terminate."*

What kind of joy could this be but that of the spirit, the promised reward of human pain? The superficial tone of the *Proemio* gives way here to an atmosphere which is edifying, medieval and solemn: *"Dico*

[2] Frye, pp. 52-53, 56-57.

adunque che già erano gli anni della fruttifera Incarnazione del Figliuolo di Dio al numero pervenuti di mille-trecento-quarantotto, quando nella egregia città di Fiorenza..."

And then the plague descends, with such *copia* of language, such shock of adjective, lamentation of phrase and sudden eruption of description, such piling of ghastly detail upon detail that all of the rest of the *Decameron* is in fact an anticlimax. This is realism expressed with such artistry that it seems to turn into allegory. There is no reason to believe that Boccaccio meant to imply more than the actuality of this bodily sickness with all its attendant horrors—the isolation of every stricken man from his own kind, the rising tide of bestiality and terror, and finally the total disintegration of society and inexorable victory of death. Still, this passage carries the kind of supraverbal resonance which evokes symbolic images in susceptible minds. What is the meaning of this sickness which strikes at the heart of the *egregia città*? It is a question which must remain unanswered, for this is not ancient Thebes and there is no oracle to consult. Here there is nothing but the reality of the charnel-house.

From a purely literary point of view, this is a masterly preparation for the construction of Boccaccio's frame which now, like the old stereopticon, provides an illusion of depth. It is perfectly obvious to the reader that for the sake of sanity and life itself it is necessary to escape from this nightmare and find security somewhere—anywhere—with Pampinea and Emilia and their charming friends. With joy and relief he steps into the welcome enclosure and finds himself almost immediately in an enchanted spot where nobody in sight is sick or old or poor; where nature is at her most gracious, and all his companions are well-bred, clever and courteous; where he need not watch the peasants vulgarly dying in their cottages round about, nor do anything, indeed, but amuse himself from morning till night.

It would perhaps be better to use the feminine pronoun here, for this is a land designed for ladies, populated by them and controlled by their lightest wishes and appetites. The lady with the *Decameron* in her silken lap is gratified to discover this reality after the hideous dream of the plague. Before she has time to discover her error, the author has begun to inject some raw vigor into this static vision—but gently at first, very gently, so that the illusion of comfortable beatitude is not disturbed. All of the ten young people who form the *lieta brigata* are to all appearances completely virtuous—the gentlemen perforce, according to custom, and the ladies somewhat wistfully observing the proprieties. Still, they are very thorough about this; they go to church on Sundays, say their prayers, and devoutly set apart Fridays and Saturdays for fasting, abstinence and washing their hair. This makes for a kind of well-groomed serenity in which the flames of courtly love may flicker continuously without danger or excitement—and before it begins to pall the author brings some life into the garden.

The diversions of the *brigata* begin with three tales which have become justly famous in spite of the myriads of novelle which have been written since. Boccaccio's sources here are not important; it is the treatment which is inimitable, and which sets the tone for the whole series. The world, with all its evil and hypocrisy, is admitted quietly into the sanctuary in the wake of a miniature sermon:

"...*Esso, al quale niuna cosa è occulta, più alla purità del pregator riguardando che alla sua ignoranza o allo essilio* [in hell, naturally] *del pregato, così come se quegli fosse nel suo conspetto beato, esaudisce coloro che'l priegano.*"

Obviously, this is intended to introduce an exemplum demonstrating the victory of a beneficent God over deficient human materials—very sound medieval theology, and applicable even to that incorrigible old scalawag Ser Ciappelletto—if the reader cares to apply it. During the telling of this first tale, however, it turns out to be far more amusing to watch the crowd of imbeciles praying to his rotting carcass and calling him a saint than to think any further about the matter. (Anyone who casts his vote for *purità*, however, is welcome to the privilege of betraying his own subnormal intelligence, peasant origins and total lack of humor.)

Pamfilo, who began and ended his tale in orotund periods, has acquitted himself nobly. The glibness of his doctrine and the side-splitting verisimilitude of Ser Ciappelletto's confession are beginning to lend a heady atmosphere to this little gathering, but its quality can not as yet be distinctly defined.

In the next story Neifile, following Pamfilo's lead, tells of another of God's wonders: the corruption at the heart of the Hierarchy itself can be made to show forth His glory. Abraham, after his trip to Rome, is more determined than ever to embrace Christianity—for a sharply ironic reason. Now this is not a tale at all, but an anecdote, the point of which depends upon the manner in which it is told. It is almost impossible to balance the naiveté, disillusionment and reasonable irrationality of gentle Abraham so that the bitterness of his conclusion is passed on to the listener without touching the Jew at all. Nevertheless, Neifile accomplishes this with ease. Christianity is vindicated, Abraham is a wise and holy man—and the audience is convulsed with merry derision.

Now Filomena takes her turn and tells the old story of the three rings, giving it the new twist which had come into fashion about two decades earlier. The older version had always provided one genuine ring, of great allegorical importance.[3] That was the whole point. Filomena's choice of the ambiguous ending reveals more than she knows. The story is not simply a narrative about another clever Jew, who works himself out of a tight corner by proving that one religion is just as good as another; it is a kind of touchstone. The hearer will react in accordance with his convictions. Since no one offers any comment at the conclusion of Filomena's contribution it appears that the uncommitted, tolerant attitude expressed so persuasively in this tale is accepted by her companions as a matter of course. This would be admirable if we could be sure that tolerance in these light hearts is not simply a matter of indifference.

Now at last the puzzling ambiguity of the atmosphere surrounding the *lieta brigata* becomes clear. In this select company it is good manners always to speak and act reverently with regard to *il buon Dio* and to be thoroughly informed as to the manner in which He would be running the cosmos—*if* He were running it. It is this sharp double vision which allows for explosions of laughter when illusion, like theatrical gauze, is suddenly rendered transparent, revealing the crass reality behind. Abraham's exposé of Rome would be far from amusing if it were not deliv-

[3] A. D. Lee, *The Decameron, Its Sources and Analogues* (London, 1909), p. 8.

ered with an air of childlike simplicity. He is not stupid but he is ludicrous—the involuntary mouthpiece of wit. Not one of Filomena's listeners feels the slightest kinship with him. Safely detached by means of intellect from the fools, and by the gracious framework of *cortesia* from all that is vulgar and offensive, the ten young friends have been set free by their witty creator for a limited period of time in which they may view the world without the hazards of wonder and compassion.

The fourth tale demonstrates without a doubt that the experience is to be for the most part a merry one. What could be funnier than pious hypocrisy suddenly brought to light, unless it be a little deft word-play concerning the gymnastics of *l'amor*? We must admit that Dioneo handles his material exceedingly well—first by causing his hearers to identify themselves with the young monk, "*il vigore del quale né la freschezza né i digiuni né le vigilie potevano macerare.*" Having done the best he could, he yields to nature and provides himself with an agreeable young girl—a normal adjustment, as any psychiatrist would agree. When it comes to the Abbot, however, who is not only hypocritical but old and fat, the goings-on become grotesque and consequently hilarious. It is the conduct of the protagonist which puts the cap on the story—for he proves himself to be not only far more clever than the Abbot, but exceedingly well-mannered, outwardly pious and lightning-quick with a gross double entendre blandly enfolded in the words of the Rule. This personable young man, as a matter of fact, except for the accident of Holy Orders, would fit in remarkably well as a member of the *lieta brigata* himself. It is obvious now that the clergy, exactly like the rest of mankind, can be classified; there are the clever ones and the fools. Avarice, hypocrisy and licentiousness, as revealed in subsequent tales, are simply born into the breed. These qualities form a target for satire which is almost too easy and commonplace, as Filostrato points out on the first day—a fixed target which "*mai non si muti.*"

Under these conditions a great change occurs in the supernatural world which was such a vital part of the medieval cosmos. Since the sacramental channels are uniformly foul and *il Creatore* Himself has become more of a rhetorical and social convention than a reality, the angels, the demons and the saints, far from disappearing, manifest themselves in ludicrous reverse. Ser Ciappelletto attracts his crowds of pilgrims and effects his cures; a farmer returns from the grave to tell what he has learned of Purgatory;[4] a daft little girl encounters the devil and acquires some anatomical knowledge of hell;[5] the Angel Gabriel flies by night over the canals of Venice and leaves his wings in Madonna Lisetta's room;[6] and a ghost comes knocking importunately, only to be exorcised by a quick-witted wife.[7] From these selected object-lessons it is clear that a belief in the supernatural is simply an invitation to the first trickster who comes along—and Frate Cipolla is right at hand with the Finger of the Holy Ghost and a bottle of St. Michael's sweat to prove it.[8]

The solitary exception to this state of affairs is the story of Nastagio who glimpses the spectral knight hunting down his lady with a pair of mastiffs.[9] This is a rather curious vision, for the dark rider, condemned to hell for suicide, manages to be at large on Fridays, ostensibly doing penance. A more puzzling anomaly is the fact that the naked beauty is obviously undergoing punishment for no mortal sin, but for the capital offense in the canon of courtly love—cruelty to her wooer. Through some judicial oversight, however, she too has been consigned to hell. This makes it justifiable for her knight to make a weekly habit of slitting her open in public and flinging her heart to the dogs—a procedure which he carries out with exemplary gusto and *virtù*. Nastagio is not slow in working this into a laboratory demonstration for his own reluctant dame, who capitulates forthwith. The entire feminine population of Ravenna, in fact, takes this apparition so much to heart that life becomes considerably gayer for the men.

The technique which is most noteworthy in this story is the deft way in which Boccaccio shifts the emphasis from the values of courtly love to a kind of inferno-scene, appropriating for his own purposes all its Dantean possibilities, and then—while his audience is still stunned with the sight of macerated female flesh—shifts it back again and finishes it off quickly in the style of an exemplum. The erotic and the horrible are expertly blended here with a detachment that the Romantics were never able to achieve—and the moral thus authenticated is so deliciously immoral that the author cannot resist a final jibe at the end.

[4] III,8. [5] III, 10. [6] IV, 2. [7] VII, 1. [8] VI, 10. [9] V, 8.

Premonitory dreams, too, are worthy of note in the Boccaccian world. It is exceedingly dangerous to ignore such warnings, as Margarita[10] and others within this group of stories find out. However, the one dreamer who is awakened by a visitor from the other world receives a message so mundane that the whole anecdote appears to be concocted simply to reassure nervous gentlemen who have violated a theological taboo.[11] In short, the realm from which real wonders come has apparently gone bankrupt. Messer Torello's fabulous journey in the Saladin's bed[12] is simply a convenient way of shipping home with him a few hundred pounds of excess baggage in the form of gold and jewelry. Even that miraculous January garden created by the magician for Messer Ansaldo[13] bears witness to no fairy kingdom; it is a purely material bribe, no more awe-inspiring than a hothouse stocked with camellias and asparagus. In fact, Chaucer does far better with his treatment of a similar plot (in the *Franklin's Tale*) by arranging for the removal of a few boulders. He also preserves the integrity of husband and wife, whereas Boccaccio allows them to slip into some regrettable ambiguities: Dianora in her too-realistic bargaining with the go-between, and Gilberto in his caitiff admission that his nobility springs partly from fear of the magician.

Nevertheless, most of the best stories in the *Decameron* represent such a skilful fusion of three sets of values—the vanished theological system, the rules of *amour courtois* and the precepts of disillusionment—that his means can be discovered only after careful analysis. Further comparisons with Chaucer's treatment of similar plots or themes reveal a few more of his methods; for instance, the fabliau[14] which corresponds with Chaucer's *Reeve's Tale*[15] is used in the *Decameron* for a very different effect. The motivation here centers about the love of a handsome young gentleman—not quite courtly love, for the responsive girl lacks credentials—but passion, nevertheless, which justifies all things, and the whole episode leads to its natural satisfaction. Thus the crassness of the fabliau is subtly mitigated. For Chaucer (who, in addition to pursuing his own literary purposes, is assisting the Reeve to scoff at millers) the point is the righteous retribution falling upon Symkyn. This allows the reader complete

[10] IX, 7.   [11] VII, 10.   [12] X, 9.   [13] X, 5.   [14] IX, 6.
[15] Discussed in Chapter II, as are the two other English tales mentioned below.

detachment concerning his humiliation, whereas when Boccaccio's luckless host cries, "*Pinuccio, la tua è stata una gran villania, e non so perché tu mi t'abbi a far questo,*" there is nothing to prevent the reader from morally agreeing with him (and wandering from the point) except the fleeting sensations of the night which has just been enjoyed by the other four. Even these, however, are made to vanish like a dream. A final note of wry philosophic wistfulness creeps in as the host's wife, "*ricordandosi dell'abbracciar d'Adriano, solo seco diceva d'aver vegghiato.*"

In the tale of the quick-witted Gulfardo,[16] Boccaccio presents an analogue of the *Shipman's Tale.* Here it is made clear that a woman who trades her love for money deserves to be cheated of both. The English story, in addition to illustrating well-known predilections of the clergy, provides an equally quick-witted *wife* (who loses nothing) and a rich husband whose mind is preoccupied with business and accounts. In each tale the mercenary dupe is punished, but the character shifts. The merchant's avarice is a venial grade of one of the Seven Deadly Sins, while Guasparruolo's wife is not cited for any theological lapse whatsoever; her greed is an offence against a major law in the covenant of love—and therefore, anathema.

In this tale Neifile makes clear the acceptable regulations concerning feminine virtue: "...*Ciascuna donna debbe essere onestissima e la sua castità come la sua vita guardare...*" This is Part One, which can be useful at times. "...*E questo non potendosi, così appieno tuttavia...per la fragilità nostra...*" Part Two, however, is indispensable. Since this theoretical *castità* has been proved to be a moral necessity and a practical impossibility, censure must always be reserved. The important question is not *whether*, but *why* the lady says yes. The treasure must be yielded up only at the behest of love, whose *forze grandissime* need no excuse.

This insistence upon the primacy of a well-bred, unselfish and overpowering passion, as opposed to the lust and violence of the world, is one of the paradoxical charms of the *Decameron.* Though the rewards of this love are frankly physical and its precepts run counter to those of religion, its effects (as in the case of the brutish Cimone)[17] can be uplifting and civilizing. The flame in the heart of Federigo,[18] springing

[16] VIII, I.   [17] V, I.   [18] V, 9.

from adulterous desire and leading to material ruin, nevertheless burns with steadiness and generosity far beyond the point when any results of his sacrifice may be foreseen. The gentle, radiant transformation of values here (from pride, desire and extravagance to humility, chaste devotion and dignified poverty) makes this story justly famous. Although the majority of the ideal loves described by Boccaccio are far more perfunctory, the measure of Don Federigo's faithfulness lends substance to them all.

The case of Griselda[19] which is set forth in literary fashion for the first time in the *Decameron*, is more complex. Her story is not only a Christian *exemplum* with a moral which can be squeezed into three succinct lines at the end, but a demonstration of ideal fidelity in love; the fact that Griselda is a wife rules out the covert melodrama which enlivens the adulterous romance, and leaves the author with little to do but push matters to extremes. Since Gualtieri is the absolute antithesis of the courtly lover, Boccaccio has little patience with the whole affair, and this attitude is reflected in his cardboard heroine. For no conceivable reason she changes not only her manners but her "*anima*" upon entering the palace, expressing her fortitude by means of a manufactured smile which lends little credence to her explanation that she accepts everything imposed upon her by God and by her husband. It may be that the artificiality in the tone of this tale stems from the fact that such submission makes little sense in a world ruled by Fortune and by a more exciting kind of love. At any rate, Gualtieri is simply one of those who are "*più degni di guardar porci che d'avere sopra uomini signoria*" and Griselda's record-breaking patience fails to make any connection with reality. (When Dioneo concludes by suggesting what a different type of wife would have done had *she* been driven out in her chemise, the whole construction comes down to earth with a salutary thump.)

In Chaucer's *Clerk's Tale*, however, the unworldly atmosphere of the stable of the Nativity is pervasive from beginning to end. It is evoked by a specific reference to the "litel oxes stalle" and hovers over Griselda herself in just such an enclosure, recurring in a similar reference later on and enfolding her when she sits "meeke and still" as a lamb when her

[19] X, 10.

38

first child is taken away. Hers is no unaccountable acquisition of good manners; she is shown from the beginning to be exceptionally devout and is simply granted a bit of extra grace to help her to endure Walter. This spiritual blooming in the palace takes the form of ladylike *gentilesse* as well as superhuman patience. It is clear from innumerable passages that her submission is rooted in faith; Walter is an earthly trial and her love is that of the saint for the scourge. If she can submit thus, points out the author conscientiously, man can certainly submit to God without knowing His reasons.

The same combination of graceful language, gentle humanity and radiance which make the *Prioress's Tale* a literary gem is evident here, but the story is weakened by the ambiguous nature of the heroine's trial—for Chaucer's Griselda would have shone to far better advantage in a convent cell. His version of the story (which is more medieval in spirit and more modern in its characterization of the protagonist than that of Boccaccio) may have left the author with an uneasy sense that even as an exemplum it depicts a deplorable human waste. If this be so, it explains the Clerk's rakish and disillusioned Envoy, which clears the atmosphere exactly as does Dioneo's personal conclusion in the Italian version—by a burst of merriment. Husbands, beware! This Griselda is simply an ideal—dead and buried—and in the real world every wife is equipped with sufficient means to make her helpmeet "wepe and wrynge and waille."

In addition to the many stories of subtly ambiguous effect—Boccaccio's masterpieces, which in this respect have never been equalled—the *Decameron* provides a number of fabulous but unmagical adventures, well spiced with illicit love and melodrama. All of these show human lives drawn from aristocratic backgrounds, tossing like matchsticks on a stormy sea of events. In the realm of the baser folk—the scalawags, peasants and dolts—the *beffe* and *burle* provide continuous entertainment. These are usually marital tricks, often involving the ubiquitous friars; their simplicity and humor depend upon the view that one who carries off a coup successfully is automatically justified. Below this sardonic and lively surface, however, there lies another level, rarely revealed in such stories, but set forth with shocking clarity in the tale of Martellino,[20] where we see the same fortuitous jumble of happenings, the same unutterable helplessness of human beings in the midst of a corrupt and rapacious society that are evident in the tales of *cortesia*.

The tenth day is reserved for stories of generosity and *magnificenzia*, which are particularly interesting because of the set of ideal values which they set forth—principles which sometimes supersede avarice, self-seeking and even *l'amore* itself. The first four are set on a rising scale: a monarch fails to reward a faithful knight but makes up for it in grand style, tossing in among assorted gifts his crown, orb and scepter.[21] (This is a fairly low grade of *magnificenzia*, since kings are expected to operate in this fashion, especially when they have the means.) Next, an abbot requites the liberal behavior of a romantic outlaw, reconciling him with the Pope.[22] (Although this is a real miracle, coming from a cleric, it actually costs him nothing, as Lauretta points out.) In the third story Nathan defends his title of the most generous man imaginable by offering a jealous rival his very life. (Here it can be seen very clearly that this kind of nobility is simply an advanced form of competition. Pride is at the heart of the matter, and champions determined not to be outdone may shed blood, exactly as in a lesser cause.) In this story Nathan finally becomes subtly ironic, embracing the murderous Mitridanes and commending the *altezza dello animo* of one who is determined not to amass money, but to spend it, and to kill—not thousands, but only one.

It is Messer Gentil, however, who, having rescued his lady from the grave, takes first prize so far in the opinion of the *brigata*.[23] A moderate degree of necrophilia is fairly common among Renaissance lovers, and in this case it is of course justified by the fact that she turns out to be alive—and pregnant. In due time Messer Gentil restores infant and lady, intact, to the original husband, having first proved his legal right to keep them both. Although we have his own assurance, attested by Lauretta, that he is still devoured by passion, the modern reader is not moved by this sacrifice; he may even be tempted to speculate as to whether day-by-day familiarity and a lusty baby might not tone down the most ardent desires and pave the way for the grand renunciation scene so effectively staged by Messer Gentil.

[20] II, I.   [21] X, I.   [22] X, 2.   [23] X, 4.

40

This story lacks universal and lasting appeal because of the artificiality of the courtly love convention upon which the sacrifice depends. A similar weakness may be seen in the two tales concerning monarchs who resist temptation, since the rights of kings over budding girls have been curtailed to some degree since the fourteenth century. In spite of this fact, however, one of the narratives soars above its limitations. In the other[24] the *magnificenzia* is balanced by absurdity, since the monarch is old, and even by current standards should know better than to fall in love with a pair of twins. King Pietro, however, is much wiser,[25] although to a disillusioned eye he might seem to have no real choice. He is confronted by a romantically addled child, but the Queen seems always to be in sight. Self-restraint, whether voluntary or simply expedient, is the only solution, but it is the courtesy and paternal tenderness shown by Pietro toward the lovesick Lisa which make this tale outstanding. The touching delicacy and grace with which he exacts his single token kiss and the fidelity and imagination with which he plays the romantic game of becoming her knight could grace a children's story. This novella, however, is intended for highly sophisticated adults who can relish the most unvarnished cynicism and lubricity without ever relinquishing their vision of an ideal realm of innocence and ceremony. Here the daughter of an apothecary may dare to love a king, while the whole glittering pageant of *cortesia* unites to preserve her sweetness unblemished and make her childish dream come true.

It is this world with which Tennyson falls in love poetically after a span of five centuries, and into which he tries to infuse more spiritual coherence than its elusive, dreamlike atmosphere can sustain. In the Cinquecento its laws and customs are set forth systematically in *Il Libro del Cortegiano*, the handbook of a fading ideal, and its spirit is given supreme literary expression in the *Faerie Queene*. We have seen the manner in which Chaucer's Knight and Squire evoke it nostalgically amid the clatter of a corrupt material world, but Boccaccio's *lieta brigata* actually create it for their own delectation during their serenely fugitive existence in the *Decameron*. It is this ideal retreat which provides the security of the group—and of their whole age—a provisional sanctuary

[24] x, 6.   [25] x, 7.

which they enliven by projecting a series of cinematic pictures of real
life or of more fantastic dreams. Out of the hundred which mark the
days of the *Decameron* there are many which fill their listeners with mirth
or with delight, and almost none which might move them to contemplation or to tears.

Since the foundation of this retreat is aesthetic, the creator may include
in its decorations anything he likes—and in the Renaissance this almost
automatically includes personages wearing togas or Athenian draperies
over their contemporary dress, or denizens of Olympus who amicably
share the cosmos with the Trinity. When Boccaccio wrote the *Decameron*
he was far more interested in the actions of human beings than in outworn deities of any extraction; hence its outstanding classical tale,
appearing near the end of the tenth day, extols an old Roman virtue.
His treatment of the firm friendship between Titus and Gisippus[26] is as
artistically persuasive as that of the erotic tales and promises at first to
remain true to the principles of fidelity, restraint and fortitude which
underlie the ideal of masculine friendship.[27] Given the assurance of
Gisippus that it is much easier to find a wife than a friend, the reader
may watch the transfer of Sofronia like so much baggage if he does not
puzzle over the fact that Titus seems to be afflicted with a clear case of
amour courtois. The lady, who is never consulted, is more philosophic,
and *"come savia, fatta della necessità virtù, l'amore il quale aveva a Gisippo
prestamente rivolse a Tito, e con lui se n'andò a Roma...."* This should wind
up the whole affair, since Titus' speech in the temple is a masterpiece of
rhetoric and self-esteem; Gisippus takes the palm for generosity, but his
friend is worthy of the sacrifice, and is ready to prove it. An elevated
kind of personal competition now ensues, in which each friend does his
utmost to die for the other; the plot becomes wildly entangled and it
requires a stroke of fortune to extricate them both and marry off Gisippus
to Titus' sister, who suddenly appears as an extra dividend.

Something has obviously happened here to the virile old Roman

[26] x, 8.

[27] This ideal suffered no competition with the love of women, which was not on the same
plane. As a matter of fact, "the ancients normally regarded it [the latter] as a vice, and this
view they passed on to the church fathers, who remained... stanch supporters of the classic
tradition." Maurice Valency, *In Praise of Love* (New York, 1958), p. 15.

spirit and the ideals governing an intellectual and spiritual union which takes precedence over any other human tie. *"Le sacre leggi della amicizia,"* lacking any real basis for sanctity, have given way to a ruling passion. If the tale had come from the pen of a rebellious young nineteenth-century poet it could be classified at once as an example of romantic subjectivity. The two friends (now Godfrey and Theodore) find refuge from a materialistic world in one another; Theodore's mad love for his friend's fiancée is part of the pattern—not to mention Godfrey's marriage to his friend's sister, which is so Byronically close to incest. At the hands of a modern writer the situation would doubtless become more sinister, and the basic relationship would be further stripped of communication and meaning. The major emphasis might well be placed upon the dreary amorality with which the protagonists (now Goupillon and Tourterelle, a cutpurse and scavenger in the gutters of Paris) live out their sterile mutual bondage as best they may.

Boccaccio, too, like authors of all times, unconsciously infuses into his material the values of his age.[28] His Titus, speaking like a Roman, behaves like a courtly lover—first with Sofronia (when the friends are comparable to Chaucer's Palamon and Arcite in the tower) and then with Gisippus. Since the intellectual detachment necessary for classical masculine friendship is not a characteristic of his period, the relationship in his novella becomes a diverting monomania—passionate, wildly impractical and sustained with superhuman tenacity to the point of death. Its only flaw is that it makes no sense. Thus we see that although there is nothing like an ideal to add zest and vigor to human existence, it must be rooted in a social or religious continuum lying beyond the private concerns of the individual or it will degenerate into an aberration. Even so, Boccaccio's Titus and Gisippus are far more healthy characters than the pallid and suicidal Godfrey and Theodore—who in turn are robust good fellows in comparison with Goupillon and his slinking mate. Without the unifying power of an ideal which not only

[28] He did not take his tale directly from a classical narrative, but uses the trappings and supplies an atmosphere which he likes better. He may have followed the 13th-century poem of courtly love ascribed to Bernay; if so, the choice indicates his preference; there were plenty of standard friendship stories available. Louis Sorieri, *Boccaccio's Story of Tito e Gisippo in European Literature* (New York, 1937), pp. 6, 21, 24.

unites the dual nature of man, but binds him in wholesome unity with all his kind, human nature turns in upon itself—as modern writers continue to demonstrate with varying degrees of apathy and gloom.

Boccaccio's world still abounds in vitality and zest because there, while the mind assents gaily to the body's delight it can also, upon demand, transcend the physical and force that body to forego its satisfactions for the sake of a human love or loyalty. Such unselfish relationships are always fruitful; the offspring is energy and hope. Although the structure upon which these ideal unions depend may be shaky and is in some instances patently outworn, their vigor animates the *Decameron*. All purely selfish, crass and hypocritical behavior is shown to be ridiculous in comparison; hence the realistic tales serve as contrast, contributing to the feeling of peaceful well-being within the ideal retreat.

Characters in such a world remain generic, for they must represent sympathetic types and their antitheses. Thus it is difficult to distinguish one of Boccaccio's young lovers from all the rest—or the responsive maidens, hypocritical monks, conniving wives and husbands, jealous mistresses and brutish peasants from their counterparts in other tales. Even the celebrated Federigo is memorable chiefly by virtue of his falcon and Ser Ciappelletto, that catalogue of sins, because of his posthumous effects. Chaucer leaves us with some far more memorable personalities, but they too are types. He takes great pleasure in clothing them in particular flesh, just as he delights in dressing the Carpenter's Alison in crisp black and white from head to foot and seeing that her ribbons match her collar.

Boccaccio, too, can be particular when he likes—for example, in his description of the kitchen maid Nuta: "*grassa e grossa e piccola e mal fatta, con un paio di poppe che parevan due ceston da letame e con un viso che parea de' Baronci, tutta sudata, unta e affumicata*"[29] or of the fresh young daughters of Messer Neri, dripping wet in their sheer white linen as they step out of the fish-pool.[30] Nevertheless, individual natures and characters are for the most part unimportant to him, even in the frame-story where, after ten days with his *brigata* we can distinguish the gay and impudent Dioneo (by his speech and actions rather than his appearance)

[29] VI, 10.   [30] X, 6.

and practically no one else. With the appurtenances of gracious living, however, he takes infinite pains, down to the very glasses, rinsed in clear water before they are placed on napery as white as snow. The manner of life led by the ten shadowy story-tellers is shared with the reader with a kind of sensuous *liberalità* devoted to arousing a train of cultivated appetites—all of which promise to converge supremely in *l'amore*.

This physical zest bubbles through most of the stories, and in the fabliaux finds an outlet in vivid word-pictures showing comic variations in that incessant human activity which provides the subject-matter for them all. Here the author's elegant style frequently turns into salty peasant dialogue innocent of euphemism—but never for so long that it cannot be given an extra fillip by some unexpected turn of speech which detaches the reader from the sordid situation and renders it more ludicrous than ever. Thus Giannello in the tale of the wine-barrel[31] is immortalized at the crucial moment by a poetic simile which brings to mind a fiery, snorting image of "*gli sfrenati cavalli e d'amor caldi...di Partia.*"

After comic ironies and sensuous delights, Boccaccio most enjoys portraying *magnificenzia* in its material form. Messer Torello in the care of the Saladin[32] is all but suffocated with gifts—wound up first in a turban of regal length and finally anchored down with a priceless buckle, of no particular use but groaning with pearls, and a mighty "*carbunculo, tanto lucente che un torchio.*" Lest these souvenirs seem inadequate, the Saladin then sets up about Torello's sleeping figure a sumptuous still-life arrangement including basins filled with double ducats, all set off tastefully against the cushions of velvet and cloth-of-gold.

Let no one censure the perspicacious *novelliere* who works out those glittering details; he is not indulging childish fancy but building a monument to his age. Even the saintly Sir Thomas More, nearly two centuries later, acknowledges the importance of "magnificence" in his society, and shows some ironic concern about the lack of it in his Utopia.[33] Besides, Boccaccio is writing for the delectation of ladies—born

[31] VII, 2.   [32] X, 9.
[33] Sir Thomas More, *Utopia*, trans. Ralph Robynson (New York, 1935), p. 158. Sir Thomas ridicules the foppish dress and ornamentation of his time, and makes gold and silver a badge of servitude in his commonwealth.

too early to wander through the modern palaces of trade and feast their eyes upon counters laden with splendors of this very kind; what now must be constructed in factories, out of synthetic metals and colored glass, he can create in his day by means of words alone—and all of his gems are real.

For a literary artist with such sensuous preoccupations the choice and arrangement of words are of primary importance; he must evoke sensations through their very sound. If he is also analytical he will fashion meticulous structures combining sound, image, logic and connotation; and if in addition he is a lover of the Latin classics, his style will reflect the dignity, elegance and decorum of his models. All of these elements are combined in the style of the *Decameron*—which is even more impressive when one realizes that Boccaccio was wrestling with the vernacular in prose and subduing it for the first time to the discipline of form.[34] The result is a "stupendous monument,"[35] not only to himself but to his age. The impulses which led him to dignify the common tongue, to enclose in fair phrases the vulgar and the comic as well as the noble and to create out of a hundred odds and ends of narrative a lively, unregenerate world rejoicing in form and beauty—these were in the atmosphere, and he absorbed them more completely than any other writer of his time. The means by which he perpetuated them are vitality and style—and "if style is a vocabulary, it is also syntax; and syntax expresses the way in which a society feels, responds, thinks, communicates, dreams, escapes."[36]

Style, however, would not be sufficient to make this master inimitable. The reality which emanates from the *Decameron* as a whole (but not from every part considered separately) is rooted in a particular facility: his capacity for writing *as if* the fundamental spiritual verities of the Middle Ages were valid to him and to his audience. Using this *as if* for a substratum, he builds a complicated structure and then devotes all of

[34] Maurice Valency, in lecture-notes for his course in the Renaissance at Columbia University, 1959.
[35] Francesco De Sanctis, *History of Italian Literature*, trans. Joan Redfern (New York, 1931), I, 356.
[36] Wylie Sypher, *Four Stages of Renaissance Style* (Garden City. New York, 1955) p. 16.

his efforts to pointing out how delightfully well it holds up without a foundation. Reading these tales is thus like watching a number of elegant human beings going in and out of a palace based on pillars which are not there. So real is this pleasure-dome, and so full of diversions, that the spectacle does not seem to be in the least ridiculous, even to the stairway which leads from the ground to the upper floors and which is made of mist. There is one glorious absurdity, however, and that is the view from the palace windows, which reveals the stupid groundlings trying to lean against the pillars or to clamber up bodily, under the illusion that they lead to heaven—and tumbling down time and time again into their native mud.

Such an impressive edifice, however, could never have been erected without those very columns, whose majestic firmness, despite the architect's scoffing, partakes of something more than vacuity. How can he know, in the midst of his merriment, that they will one day appear as solid to Giovanni Boccaccio himself as to one of his most credulous simpletons? Their reality, which has been lying in the eye of the beholder for centuries of human faith and incredulity, upholds the world of the *Decameron* precisely in those places where it seems to be least supported. From this fact springs the powerful attraction of that realm, laid open so seductively by art and wit to the senses, but informed by a mysterious wholeness beyond the control of the skeptic who created it—a Spirit which, having been more than once ironically invoked in this little world, refuses as serenely to be banished as to come into view.

CHAPTER FOUR

THE MERRY HALF-WORLD OF DES PÉRIERS: LES NOUVELLES RÉCRÉATIONS ET JOYEUX DEVIS

The influence of the *Decameron*, spreading slowly at first, worked its way through Italy and reached its peak in the Cinquecento. After the lapse of two centuries the countless diligent novellieri, whether Tuscans, Lombards or Venetians, were still reflecting in their tales a series of duller or more fragmentary images of Boccaccio's world. And still the dominion of the *lieta brigata* widened and spread, finally crossing the mountains to the north and finding a royal welcome in the miniature kingdom of Navarre.

Here, as in Italy, the immediate effect of the hundred tales was literary imitation. Queen Marguerite herself, the royal poetess who, for all her mystical transports, was not above repeating an earthy anecdote, began to collect what was intended to be her own Decameron. Her young secretary, Bonaventure des Périers, likewise a poet and likewise graced with courtly *joie de vivre*, did the same. Both, however, although they were attracted by the suave Italian polish, remained proudly and exclusively French; both were intellectual realists, valiantly struggling to retain their hold on crumbling ideals. The world taking shape in their nouvelles required a union of irreconcilables. The Italian pattern of *cortesia*, so civilized and seductive to the French, could no longer be preserved within a garden; it was threatened, not by a plague but by a fire.

Throughout northern Europe the flames of religious fanaticism, now Catholic, now Protestant, had ravaged court and countryside alike. The odor of the faggot and the voices of heretics subjected to the refinements of the *estrapade* penetrated palace windows and carried the sharp reminder that there was no sure safety anywhere. Human beings of intelligence and probity were moved to meditate, to question and to seek new answers to the problems of faith and reason in the emergent vision of Reform. Marguerite and her circle of celebrities exerted a magnetism which proved irresistible to the rootless young Des Périers, trained in independent thought. He came, he saw, he listened and was entranced. Figures whose very names now epitomize an era—Rabelais, Calvin—provided constant intellectual stimulation and personal drama. The atmosphere of Lyon was one of fiery idealism, controversy, and mounting tension—all set off by a spirit of badinage, galanterie and literary grace crystallized for posterity in each new lyric issuing from the pen of Marot.

Des Périers himself was possessed of greater than ordinary gifts in more than one area of expression, and has been compared with his friend and model Marot as well as with Rabelais and Voltaire. Before we can determine his position among the outstanding tellers of tales it is necessary to decide whether or not he suddenly lost his faith (and with it, the whole upper story of his literary cosmos), or whether his prose dialogues and the nouvelles reflect a *suppression* of one half of his nature for reasons more complex; it is no accident that in his merriest mood it does not appear at all.

His versatility, characteristic of his age, was an attractive trait in the young poet who called himself "Dedalus" and yearned lyrically for the romantic abbess Claude de Bectoz[1] and perhaps, in the opinion of at least one critic, for Marguerite herself.[2] Moved by the mystic fervor of his Queen, he not only copied out for her the effusions of her soul, but followed suit with his own translations of the Psalms and Canticles and such evangelical works as the *Prognostication des Prognostications* (1536), fired with zeal and the sense that he was helping to free his countrymen from the intellectual lethargy imposed by meaningless Latin and coun-

---

[1] Adolphe Chenevière, *Bonaventure des Périers, sa vie, ses poésies* (Paris, 1886), pp. 76-78.
[2] Bonaventure des Périers, *Le Cymbalum Mundi, précédé des Nouvelles Récréations et Joyeux Dévis*, ed. P. L. Jacob (Paris, 1858), p. xlvi.

teracting the oppressions of the Hierarchy. Since his education had been conducted under the guidance of the liberal abbé de St. Martin[3] and his early literary apprenticeship had included assistance to Pierre Olivetan in the translation of the Waldensian Bible,[4] religion had always formed the circumference if not the center of his life. It is impossible to doubt his personal sincerity in these writings—an integrity attested by innumerable letters and lyrics addressed to the Queen—but he was no fanatic. He was likewise no mystic, and thus lacked the spiritual resources which sustained Marguerite in the face of the dread realities of gibbet and block set up in the name of Christianity.

In self-defence he employed his analytical, witty and classically-educated mind to search for *la vérité*, and located her in the Antipodes, trying vainly to burrow her way through the earth to reach the Christians busily setting up barricades against her.[5] Proceeding with a Voltairean lightness and éclat which set off a bitter vision (couched in terms foreshadowing the obfuscations of Swift) he wrote the four audacious dialogues comprising *Le Cymbalum Mundi*. Critical opinion concerning this ferocious little work was as varied in his own time as it is today; it is possible to trace in its allegory of contemporary religious issues the opinions of an atheist and blasphemer, but it is quite as reasonable to view it as the work of a disenchanted scholar and wit setting forth "*la ridicule comédie des croyants de son temps, qu'il voit tous s'appuyer d'une main sur l'autel de l'autre sur l'échafaud.*"[6]

Nevertheless, the book was burnt by order of Parliament, along with a certain luckless librarian, Jehan de la Garde, who had bought a copy from the printer. The judgment rendered subsequently by the Faculty of Theology of the Sorbonne upon suppressing this incendiary little work was ambiguous: "*Nous le supprimons bien qu'il ne contienne pas d'erreurs expresses en matière de foi, mais parce qu'il est pernicieux.*" Meanwhile, a reader of the *Cymbalum* had gone to the stake while the author, presumably because of his court connections, went unscathed.[7]

[3] Chenevière, p. 13.　　[4] Ibid., pp. 28–9.
[5] *Cymbalum Mundi*, Dialogue IV.
[6] Bonaventure des Périers, *Oeuvres Françaises*, ed. Louis Lacour (Paris, 1856), p. lxii, quoted in Chenevière, p. 62.
[7] Chenevière, pp. 65–66.

This ironic state of affairs could not continue very long. The scandal caused by this unexpected satire from the pen of a protégé of the Queen finally cost him his position at court—since Marguerite was having more than enough difficulty in maintaining her own indefinable balance between the old faith and the new. If her devoted secretary had indeed become a total unbeliever and libertine, the change had apparently occurred with the suddenness of a thunderclap. However, the faith of a lifetime may seep away slowly, but rarely explodes in a negative direction. This is all the more reason for concluding that the *Cymbalum Mundi* expresses nothing more "*pernicieux*" than the disillusion of an intelligent, idealistic young man who could not become inured to the spurt of blood and the odor of burning flesh, even in the name of Reform; one who, having arisen one day from a debilitating attack of the fever,[8] found the connection between faith and reason temporarily suspended. The gay and witty tone of the Dialogues bespeaks a stable base below the surface —and where could such security lie for Bonaventure des Périers? Not, as for Boccaccio, in an artificial structure based upon *cortesia*, nor, as for Chaucer, in the faith of his country and of his age—because neither possibility existed for a literary man in the France of 1538, half medieval, half fanatical and cruelly torn. Even if he had been born two centuries later he would have been no cool rationalist like Voltaire, condensing into philosophical *contes* his gifts of satire, imagination and style. The temperament of Marguerite's young poet was more complex, and what sustained him was the atmosphere emanating from that remarkable court in which, over a substratum of ancient faith, three separate modes of thought and feeling were combined: evangelical fervor, skeptical humanism and the religion of love. It was the new Platonism which for a time offered the promise of containing all the rest in a glorious synthesis. Cut off from its source through his own integrity or stubbornness (for he ignored diplomatic warnings concerning the *Cymbalum*)[9] Des Périers could not longer exist; he perished in a short time—probably by his own hand.[10]

[8] Ibid., p. 58.   [9] Ibid., p. 67.
[10] James W. Hassel, Jr., *Sources and Analogues of the Nouvelles Récréations et Joyeux Devis* (Chapel Hill, N.C., 1957), p. 21.

Critics disagree concerning the quality of his skepticism, but from the standpoint of psychology and common sense it is unlikely that a youth who could be moved to spiritual exaltation at his first sight of the Queen in a penitential procession would, within two years, abjure all faith, flaunt his atheism in print and jeopardize his career and his very life. Thoroughgoing rationalists are more canny and circumspect. Tilley finds in the fourth Dialogue some basis for concluding that the author is actually expressing sympathy for primitive Christianity and giving a veiled warning concerning the wisdom of keeping silent about heretical opinions.[11] Lefranc also sheds light on the problem when he describes the position of the *modérés*—members of the third (but unofficial) religious faction, who, without sacrificing their idealism, rejected the portion of Protestant dogma which was incompatible with their "*rêve de tendresse et de liberté.*" Among these "*libertins spirituels*" he includes Rabelais, Dolet and Des Périers.[12] Without understanding the sensitive and equivocal nature of this position, no critic can discover a satisfactory relationship between the *Récréations* and the rest of Des Périers' work. This dilemma confronted literary commentators in the later sixteenth century as well as all who followed them.

It is not only the puzzling geographical discrepancies which seem to rule out the poet as the author of the merry tales—for these can be easily explained as the result of later interpolations;[13] it is the marked difference between the spirit of this collection and the tone of the *Cymbalum.* This so impressed the logical Abbé Jugé that he constructed a thesis upon it in 1907, employing not only the arguments of the earlier critics, but also a good deal of close textual analysis and comparison. In spite of the fact that his conclusions were discredited by Sainéan and Becker,[14] and that the authorship of the *Récréations* is no longer seriously questioned, Jugé's study clarifies an important point which is not the main concern of his critique: the fact that the nouvelles are enclosed in an atmosphere which is uncontroversial and medieval, and that their author (Peletier, as he seeks to prove) "*finit, avec un chef d'œuvre, le moyen*

---

[11] Arthur Tilley, *The Literature of the French Renaissance* (New York, 1959) I, p. 128.
[12] Abel Lefranc, *Grands Ecrivains Français de la Renaissance* (Paris, 1914), p. 79.
[13] Hassell, p. 26.   [14] Ibid.

âge."[15] The *Cymbalum*, on the other hand, he ascribes to another kind of writer altogether—one who sounds like an atheist, shows contempt for ritual and condemns the spectacle of theology stooping to violence in order to enforce that which cannot be proved.[16] This spirit, of course, places the satire in one age and the *nouvelles* in another—an apparent anomaly, since the tales, according to the author himself, were written over an extended period which doubtless included the year in which the *Cymbalum* appeared. Even when Jugé takes the *Récréations* away from Des Périers and gives them to Peletier, there remains a disparity between the satire and all of Des Périers' other work, and the honest critic is still forced to concede that this writer spans two cultures in a remarkable fashion.[17]

This is the crucial point in our analysis of the quality of the *Récréations*. All of the foregoing considerations are important if we are to accept the critical assumption that Des Périers actually wrote the *nouvelles* attributed to him, for our task will then be to relate the merry world which is reflected there with the separate realms of his poetry and of the satire.

Jugé has noted that the tales offer a view which is concrete, balanced and optimistic as contrasted with that of the *Cymbalum*, which is abstract, rhetorical and infused with a suicidal melancholia.[18] While it is true that Des Périers, from all reports, ended his own life—perhaps with a kind of desperate flourish appropriate to his own bizarre seigneur de Vaudrey[19]—it seems likely that this deed resulted from the sudden severance of the lifeline which joined him to the Court. The disgrace occurred *after* the publication of the *Cymbalum*, which in tone and wit is about as gloomy as *Candide*, and as suicidal as the mood of Gulliver upon escaping from the lovesick little yahoo on the riverbank. Christian Europe, as reflected in the four dialogues, is one vast joke, and the supernatural confusion mirrored in its theology is more ludicrous still. The writer who can portray Luther and Calvin[20] as talking dogs and render a tavern scene with Mercury having a little *vin de Beaulne* with the boys

---

[15] Clement Jugé, *Jacques Peletier du Mans (1517-1582), essai sur sa vie, son œuvre, son influence* (Paris, 1907), p. 417.
[16] Ibid., p. 293.   [17] Ibid., p. 327.   [18] Ibid., pp. 296-297.   [19] Nouvelle LV.
[20] Or Rabelais and Dolet. Critics disagree as to their exact identity.

down in Athens is obviously not a victim of despair; he is viewing his world in a new and liberating light.

Ebullient humor also fills the ninety nouvelles which the critics now allot to the author of the *Cymbalum*, although its source in the tales is quite different. It bubbles forth, not at the spectacle of man's spiritual blindness and the consequent frustrations of *la vérité*, but at human weakness, pretension and stupidity in the material world. This is the familiar realm of the fabliaux, attached to no supernatural structure whatsoever, and populated with dolts going through the motions pre-scribed by a hypocritical clergy. The amoral law of cause and effect is not so finely balanced as it is in Chaucer's merry tales because of the quantity of the *Récréations et Joyeux Devis*; still, it functions dependably and becomes ambiguous only in rare moments when the author allows a trace of human sympathy to creep in (as in the sixty-first nouvelle, when the son of a thief is hanged through a clerical mistake, and the ninetieth, which shows a cuckold drowning his wife in the river). Elsewhere, the detachment is as strict as in the most rigid exemplum, which is of course the secret of the humor. This is a world of common fellows who are ridiculous in speech, habits and naiveté; they are also, because of the detail with which their mannerisms are set forth, unmis-takably French.[21] If by chance we run across some gentler folk in this collection they are almost always gay caricatures like the daft seigneur de Vaudrey who tested out his armor by running at an unsheathed sword with all his might, and strangled a cat *"a belles dentz,"*[22] or the self-conscious ladies who talked of nothing but their diets.[23] It is not the manners of the court which are held up to ridicule here, but silly ex-aggerations of polite ideals. This marks a new turn in the nouvelle, and demonstrates the same salutary impudence shown by Molière when he began to bring fops and *précieuses* into his comedies.

The code of the fabliau, however, prevails over all, and is most clearly demonstrated in the world of thieves and scoundrels. It allows a cutpurse to make off with a priest's money-bag, for the curé has obviously been selling wheat belonging to the Church, but firmly approves the hanging

---

[21] In spite of the fact that the sources are varied, and are by no means confined to France.
[22] Nouvelle LV.   [23] LVII.

54

of that same thief for robbing the man who made his knife.[24] The only moral in the whole collection which is not based upon expediency is illustrated by Blondeau, the jolly cobbler who throws away his pot of money in order to be happy; but this is shown to be so surpassingly practical a move on his part that no one would dare to call him an idealist.[25]

Practical knowledge is, in fact, of prime importance in this world, and the nouvelles abound in demonstrations of how to do everything from curing a somnambulist[26] to making a monkey cut its own throat.[27] Even the large percentage of salacious anecdotes and repartee represents an aspect of this same practicality in an area of universal interest; the tales provide object-lessons, exactly as if the audience had asked particular questions: How may a lady effectually rebuke her spouse for sleeping the whole night through?[28] What would happen if an enterprising young fellow managed to enter a convent in disguise? And what could he do if the Mother Superior finally decided to put on her glasses?[29] Is reluctance actually a hallmark of virginity?[30] Could a kiss become a matter for the law?[31]

In addition to specific illustrations there are also set forth in the last tale attributed to Des Périers[32] some general principles concerning feminine virtue, errant wives and the varieties of cuckoldry. A curious new note is sounded amid these familiar strains of disillusion, however, when the author, suddenly assuming a more personal tone, exposes the sham Platonism current in his own milieu. *"La vertu spirituelle,"* he points out, is quite a different thing from *"cette vertu substantifique et humorale"* which provides diversion for an amorous Court. In ideal love *"il suffit de joindre les espritz ensemble...."* This pronouncement, coming at the end of eighty-nine uninhibited *récréations et joyeux devis* has an effect rather like that of Chaucer's *Retractation*—but not for long. This is a philosophic note which has been struck, and its resonance has no religious overtones;

---

[24] LXXIX.   [25] XIX.   [26] XLI.   [27] XIXb.   [28] XXXII.

[29] LXII.   [30] XXXIX.   [31] LXXVIII.

[32] Tilley questions the authorship of this 90th nouvelle, but if it is indeed the last in Des Périers' collection, its position presents a valid reason for the change in tone: here the teller of tales changes back into the idealistic courtier for a moment before bidding his audience adieu.

it carries no farther than a paragraph. Having duly restored the ideal to its pedestal, Des Périers moves on to the evils of mercenary love, then shifts back adroitly into his customary mood of merry disillusionment. He can now finish his tale, which sets forth one practical method of dealing with an unfaithful wife. To drown her may appear "*un peu cruelle et inhumaine. Mais que voulez-vous? Il fasche à un mari d'estre cocu en sa propre personne.*"

The author of the *Récréations*, like Boccaccio, demonstrates an unflagging interest in matters erotic, a fondness for practical jokes and a peculiar sensitivity to language. Des Périers, however, does not confine the latter trait to style alone, but allows it to become part of his subject-matter as well; he deliberately chooses a number of anecdotes and longer pieces which depend for effect upon the use of words, in addition to the simple puns and *bons mots* which he tosses in generously, sometimes in sets of two or three, out of sheer *joie de vivre*. Those aspects of language which are decried in the nouvelles include artificial scholarly jargon used to impress others,[33] ecclesiastical Latin in shreds and scraps, learned by rote,[34] ambiguous legal terminology,[35] linguistic naiveté which confuses homonyms or functions only on the literal level,[36] and dialect, especially that of Poitou.[37] In addition, he creates the pseudo-scholastic term *singepedie* for the education of monkeys, and has a little fun with anagrams. The joke, however, is not at the expense of young Jehan, who works out two gay *devises* from his own name,[38] for the lad is honest and naive. A similar simplicity possesses the soul of the unlearned priest who simply repeats the name of Jesus for every Latin word which he cannot read.[39] This anecdote seems remarkably devout and touching in comparison with the others in the collection, but the reader should not be misled. Even this seemingly unwordly fellow wins the approbation of the *gentilhomme* under the old fabliau code: he is resourceful in a tight spot, he knows how to humble himself before his social superiors (witness the ridiculously repeated "*Monsieurs*" in his speech) and he does not pretend to be what he is not. These qualities, and not his parrot-like devotion, are what serve him well in the practical world of the *Récréations*.

[33] Nouvelles XIV, XXI. [34] VII, XX. [35] LXI. [36] XXXVI, XLII, XLIII.
[37] LXIX, LXX, LXI. [38] LXXIV. [39] XXII.

The infectious high spirits which enliven even the shortest of these ninety anecdotes and tales do not bubble out automatically from the material, but are an aspect of Des Périers' remarkable style. Since a great many of the nouvelles have traceable analogues or likely sources, an excellent way to measure the literary skill of their author is to examine them along with the bare bones of content in Hassell's incomplete study. Des Périers is not in the least concerned with Boccaccian periods nor with rhetoric except in minute doses, and has not bothered with a literary frame at all—simply because his method of telling a tale is dramatic. The setting is implicit in the assumption that he is actually present in a court circle, entertaining his friends. His manner is intimate, gay and confidential, and to maintain the rapport with his reader he employs innumerable witty asides, often ironic, in the form of questions, comments and exclamations. In like manner, his characters are always eager to discard their third-person existence and launch into dialogue, if only for a paragraph. This is of course the basic technique of the *facetia*, but Des Périers usually takes it further. He adds repetitions and rhymes,[40] and mimics a great variety of intonations ranging from the incoherence of feeble wit to the glib patter of the damoiselle.

When he has recourse to description he captures life in a few vivid strokes, embellishing details to the point of surprising verisimilitude— for example, the antics of the monkey in the eighty-ninth nouvelle, or the catalogue of personal qualities ascribed to the redoubtable M. Salzard in the eighty-third. Des Périers' combination of ebullience, *delicatesse* and ironic wit, laced with frankly sensual gusto, is Gallic. It lacks the comprehensiveness and flow of Chaucer and the suave, firmly-structured *copia* of Boccaccio, but rejoices in an air of highly sophisticated naïveté which is both refreshing and stimulating. Allowing for a change of pace because of the classical framework of the *Cymbalum*, one may discover it there in the dialogues, intact. Even in Des Périers' poetry these essential ingredients are a latent source of vitality. Here the naïveté is transmuted into the single-mindedness of the lover or the zealot and the sophistication is transferred from the realm of the intellect to that of form. In the prose style of the tales, however, this young writer makes his most

[40] From oral tradition, or in excellent imitation of it.

enduring mark, setting a pattern which will later be expanded to full perfection in the dialogue of Molière.

Guilelessness, whether genuine or feigned, and refinement of expression are the most effective means of mitigating the coarseness of the fabliau material and transforming it into literature. Boccaccio, Chaucer and Des Périers are all exceedingly skilful in these techniques. The Italian, however, prefers the second;[41] the Englishman, the first;[42] while the Frenchman plays with both. The methods function on the same principle—artificial infusion of the ideal into the real, which serves to raise a purely appetitive or physical situation at least one step higher in the literary scale; the resulting detachment also serves to offset the cruelty inherent in most fabliaux. Chaucer and Boccaccio never question the dénouements of their tales—but it is noteworthy that Des Périers expresses occasional doubts about the justice of events such as the hanging of an innocent boy or the drowning of a wife. Still, he neither omits these stories nor fills in circumstances (as does Chaucer) to make the human accounts balance out. This young man, restless child of the Renaissance and the Reform, is not intellectually convinced that justice and virtue can be made to jibe with the realities of human nature. In the *Cymbalum* he demonstrates cynically that they cannot be found, and in the tales he humorously throws up his hands from time to time, disclaiming the ability to figure such things out.[43] In his poetry, however, he infuses all the idealism of a sensitive, amorous and religious temperament.

If we were to pursue the treasure metaphor which allots to the *Canterbury Tales* a complete coinage and which detects in the *Decameron* superlative skill in craftsmanship and counterfeiting, we would surely identify the *Récréations* as a box of rare little coins, all of a single denomination. Their brilliant polish and varied design indicate that this artisan is adept at working finer metal; we must look outside the casket to find the proof—in the *Cymbalum*, the courtly lyrics, the Canticles, Psalms

---

[41] "..*Niuna sì disonesta n'è, che, con onesti vocaboli dicendola, si disdica ad alcuno...*." *Decameron*, p. 1066.
[42] Chaucer reserves another trick which is better still: a preternatural system of tit for tat.
[43] LXI, XC.

and religious poems. The coinage derives part of its value by the virtue of the fact that these other artifacts exist—but they are not negotiable on the same level; hence Des Périers' currency is incomplete. With the contents of his collection one may purchase only half a world.

This may indicate that in the fragmented sixteenth century a writer could no longer find a casket ample enough to contain a full currency made up of tales alone. This hypothesis will be tested in the next three chapters, but in the meantime it may be noted that the glint of steel in the *Cymbalum* corresponds to the ambiguous gleam which flickers through the major portion of the *Decameron*—the light of mockery and disillusion. Nowhere in Chaucer's box is there anything which gives back such a dubious reflection. Still, by means of his religious poetry, Des Périers rounds out and stabilizes a full scale of values. This allows him to concentrate his other resources and to restrict the *Récréations* to a single level without loss of vitality. He presents to his friends a realistic segment of life which requires no questioning and no excuse; the contrast with well-mannered existence is side-splitting; the vicarious experience is outrageous and mysteriously satisfying to his auditors, who are treated to a sensation of security and release at the same time.

In the nouvelle presenting that monster of crassness, the *"honneste monsieur"* Salzard, the ladies are shown the exact opposite of what a *gentilhomme* should be, and teased with the idea of having to take him for a husband. Without his alter ego, who remains invisible, M. Salzard would be neither comic nor alive. The spectacle of the rascal "Thoinette" at large in the house full of women is titillating because the establishment is a convent instead of a brothel. Here again the humor of the real is created through the image of the ideal.[44]

Relishing the license of the fabliau realm, Des Périers plays up its exaggerations with all the verbal skill at his command. Drunkards, gluttons and scalawags accomplish superhuman feats without disturbing the illusion of reality, for they are all types fitted out with individual

---

[44] Cross brings out this aspect of the comic with admirable clarity, showing that it depends upon a position *between* the real and the ideal, and citing the absence of humor in "out and out romances" and the work of "out and out naturalists." Wilbur Cross, *The Development of the English Novel* (New York, 1899), p. 190.

traits. So skilful is the author at detail, however, that the most threadbare anecdote appears to be an actual event which has occurred at a particular time in a familiar locality. Part of this enrichment, of course, is the result of oral tradition, impossible to distinguish from the literary additions.[45] Even if Des Périers had done nothing more with these nouvelles than to transmit them as he heard them, the result would be a remarkable achievement; he has obviously imparted to them something of himself, however, and it is this indefinable quality which places them in the top rank for their kind.

The atmosphere of the collection—almost totally medieval and totally French—has led one thoughtful critic to conclude that the real author, unlike Marguerite and Rabelais, was actually indifferent to Reform, and sought only to pacify his anxious readers by harking back nostalgically to the time of their "*aïeux.*"[46] Upon careful examination, however, the good old days depicted here appear to be filled with every manner of vice, violence and corruption, burdened with fools and plagued with knaves, with consequences ironic in the highest degree— exactly like any age seen through the lenses of the realist. The fact that the sight is humorous, however, constitutes proof that this realism is only partial; somewhere there lies the hidden contrast which evokes either laughter or tears. Des Périers has simply detached himself from the human activity portrayed in his tales.[47] This, the old fabliau convention, is the price of laughter in a frustrating world. The supersensitive young poet, who well knows how salutary sheer merriment can be, has created a little masterpiece out of the story of the sick man who is cured by laughter;[48] he has also carefully fenced in his gay domain by means of plaintive sonnets at the beginning and end. Their tone is so different from the impudent, "*Si vous n'en riez si n'en ploueray-je pas*"[49] which crystallizes the mood of the nouvelles that they offer a momentary

[45] Analogues for many of the nouvelles may be traced through other literatures, but the actual sources remain uncertain.
[46] Jugé, pp. 335-336.
[47] But not completely. Detachment becomes progressively more difficult for the novellieri, as the following chapters will attempt to show.
[48] Nouvelle LXXXIX.
[49] Nouvelle LXXXVII.

glimpse into another world—a place of aspiration, struggle and romantic defeat. The introductory verse shows "Dedalus" trying to forget for a moment the precarious flutter of his wings:

> J'ay oublié mes tristes passions,
> J'ay intermis mes occupations.
> Donnons, donnons quelque lieu a folie;
> Que maugré nous ne nous vienne saisir,
> Et en un jour plein de melancholie
> Meslons au moins une heure de plaisir.

And, at the end, he sweeps into view once more, laughing bravely in the sunshine before those pinions let him fall:

> Assez, assez, les siecles malheureux
> Apporteront de tristesse entour eux;
> Donq au bon temps prenez esjouyssance;
> Puis, quand viendra malheur vous faire effort,
> Prenez un cueur...Mais quel? Hardy et fort,
> Armé sans plus d'invincible constance.

CHAPTER FIVE

A WORLD IN SPLINTS: THE HEPTAMÉRON
OF MARGUERITE D'ANGOULÊME

The world of Bonaventure des Périers was likewise the world of his
Queen, and like him she possessed the wit, learning and poetic gift to
express that world in its divided aspects by means of several literary forms.
However, since she was more mystic than poetess, more *grande dame*
than philosopher, and, it appears, more feminine than anything else,
she discovered in her maturity the unifying key to her whole cosmos.
This was love, in an aspect totally new and yet warmly familiar, putting
an end to the warfare between flesh and spirit and making the real world
a means of reaching the ideal.

Thus equipped, she set about merrily, but with great seriousness of
purpose, to set forth a picture of that world in which nothing whatsoever
need be left out. Since this project was not initiated by a perusal of
Dante, but of Boccaccio, the task of unification, even with her Platonic
key, was a difficult one. In situations where her Italian model simply
smiled enigmatically instead of committing himself, she found it advis-
able to clarify all the moral and religious aspects in a thoroughgoing and
almost housewifely fashion—and this she could not do without a frame.
Des Périers' gay and rakish half-world, presented with no excuses and
intensely real by virtue of the fact that it was grounded on the material
plane, was not expansive enough for Her Majesty—but it was an
aspect of her own. Armed with an assortment of tales and anecdotes
gathered from friends and her own experience, as well as from oral
tradition, she provided herself with an ingenious frame and began with

the first two nouvelles to put her world in order. *L'amour*, the unifying principle, bogged down in its lowest aspects in a slough of lust and vice, finally emerges triumphantly as that love of God which can turn a poor muleteer's wife into a martyr in the cause of chastity.

This transition, however, is not effected by the events of the tales themselves, which are a welter of violence and sensationalism; it is brought about by means of comments, which thoughtfully relate these fortuitous events to their ultimate meaning. Now we begin to see that the members of the little company in her Boccaccian frame are selected for their different points of view, and that the author uses their apparently spontaneous discussions to sift the moral values of each nouvelle. Still, no comment is ever really definitive; the reader may select what he chooses. In this way Marguerite approximates the ambiguity of her model without relinquishing the privilege of directing the argument; the observations of Parlamente, her *porte-parole*, are the most elevated and sweetly reasonable in every case. Oisille, that redoubtable matriarch, obviously modeled on the mother of Francis and Marguerite, is inflexibly religious and socially correct; the other ladies, feminine, fluttery and irrational; while Simontault, Saffredent and Hircan maintain a balance of unregenerate common sense. Dagoucin, the amorous idealist, scorns mercenary concerns and talks like Bembo[1] when the author gives him a chance, but it is Parlamente whose feminine wisdom and spirituality always carry the day.

This is paradoxical, because Marguerite has from the beginning taken pains to demonstrate the utter worldliness of her milieu. The very monks of Notre Dame de Serrance, who offer a place of refuge for the company, are humorously contemptible and corrupt in the ancient tradition—skulking behind the hedge to hear the scandalous tales, forgetting vespers, and impatient to have the titled visitors gone so that they may resume their habitual peccadillos. As for the company itself, it clearly harbors hidden amours, half betrayed by coughs and blushes— innocent, perhaps, but expressed in a series of sly double entendres which hark back to the personal history of each character and hint at amorous exploits past, present and to come.

[1] Especially at the end of the 70th nouvelle.

The spirit of this little group, in fact, reflects neither the ancient medieval dualism nor the graceful idolatry of *amour courtois*, but a little of both and more than a little of something else entirely; and the common denominator of all three is the versatile term *amour*. The mystical implications in the work of Nicolas of Cusa and Ficino had found fertile ground in the soul of the Queen of Navarre, as they did in other spirits during the first stages of the Reform; there were now not only the Gospels from which to draw sustenance, but a new literary scripture, rich in Platonic borrowings and hints of *"le ravissement mystique,"* expressed in such words as these:

"L'amour estre en toutes choses, pour toutes choses, createur de toutes choses et maistre de toutes choses, — Amour est autheur et conservateur de toutes choses." [2]

When Marguerite found in this elixir a new upsurge of her traditional faith, she sang—borrowing the form and style of her own love-poets to express the ardors of her soul. As she pursued the intricacies of the new cult she discovered that medieval asceticism was no longer necessary for beatitude; the main requirement was a steady position on the escalator of love, which moves ever upward from the lowest to the highest. As she became more immersed in study and contemplation she did not cease to sing—but at the same time she turned out a collection of some of the most earthy tales and slices of court gossip ever to come out of Italy, France and Spain. Secure in the conviction that the love which animates the Boccaccian garden is separated only by degree from that in the Fourth Gospel, she drew the sundered parts of her world together by force of feminine will; in the process she accomplished what might be called a most successful sublimation for herself. She was a woman possessed of unusual powers of love, thwarted by the drab reality of life. Married twice to husbands very like the crass Hircan and Simontault, frustrated by the kind of devotion offered by a real Dagoucin and dominated throughout her life by an obsession with her royal brother, she required all of the spiritual strength which Greek idealism and evangeli-

[2] Abel Lefranc, *Grands Ecrivains Français de la Renaissance* (Paris, 1914), pp. 121-122, 162, 148.

cal zeal could give her. It is doubtless to her credit that Calvin finally turned
a frigid back upon her free flights from orthodoxy.[3] What she has left
to posterity is a radiantly human image of herself as a queen and as a deeply
spiritual woman—and inestimable service to the literature of France.

Before we assess this contribution more fully, it will be well to note
the three separate realms in which the nouvelles of her *Heptameron*
ironically subsist (escaping, as do the events of human life, all orderly
systems of cause and effect). The first is the plane of stark reality; the
second, the vanishing dream of *amour courtois*, illogical and intermittent;
the third, a world in the process of being redeemed through Christian
Platonism. When these categories have been distinguished amid the
violence and confusion, it can be seen that the entire collection and its
framework comprise a humorous moral struggle: Parlamente, assisted
by the ramrod-backed Oisille, is on one side; they are supported by the
wistful Dagoucin and—rather undependably—by the other ladies.
Their chief opponent is that thick-skinned hedonist Hircan, whose
cohorts include Simontault, Saffredent and Geburon (who, because of
his years, is gradually moving toward Parlamente's position.)[4] It
becomes clear, as the discussions proceed, that this is not only the battle
of the sexes rendered in gay banter, but a more serious conflict between
idealism and materialism. Parlamente and her allies have at stake far
more than the laurels for a few afternoons of repartee; they are fighting
for the civilization of France.

As each narrative is presented by one story-teller or another, the rest
look on, like Olympians, accepting or rejecting conclusions and then
passing final judgment—but not unanimously. The meaning of these
human events and of the world in which they take place thus depends
upon the point of view of the judges. The decision is doubly important
because almost all of the action takes place in an aristocratic setting, while
the occurrences themselves are on the fabliau level. Unless they can be
redeemed by the discussions, there can be no doubt that humor, grace,
fidelity and love itself are idle dreams. This is a region of expensive
luxuries—crimson satin doublets, Spanish horses and plump damoiselles

[3] Samuel Putnam, *Marguerite of Navarre* (New York, 1935), p. 345.
[4] Nouvelle XVII.

under thirty—all threatened by rivals, husbands, monks and murderers; its way of life is the ancient sequence of lust, trickery, rage and sudden death. To live in such a world and still retain life, wife and gusto requires a clear-cut philosophy. Of the three different points of view set forth in the *Heptameron*, that of Hircan and his supporters is by far the most frank, natural and forthright; it is constantly exposing hypocrisy and deceit in courtly mores, and for this reason is richest in humor. Some of its basic principles and precepts, distilled from the tales and discussions, are as follows:

No murderer, adulterer or robber, if he is as clever as he is wicked, is ever blamed or brought to justice. It is only stupidity that is punished—not vice.[5]

Experience shows that the mocker is mocked, the deceiver deceived and the proud man humbled.[6]

Even the best human hearts are worth nothing.[7]

"To me, it seems much better to love a woman as a woman than to make her one's idol, as many do."[8]

"Is it reasonable that we should die for women who are made only for us, and that we should be afraid of asking of them what God commands them to give us?"[9]

The concept of feminine honor did not arise until after the Golden Age, when women ceased to be able to love. "Those that could not compass ...true love said that they were forbidden by honor."[10]

"The surest way to seduce a woman is to begin by talking about honor and virtue."[11]

"Women, resisting natural love through pride, become as cruel as brutes and as crafty as devils."[12]

---

[5] Nouvelle XII (Saffredent's voice).   [6] LI (Geburon).
[7] XXI (Simontault).   [8] XIII (Saffredent).   [9] IX (Hircan).
[10] XLII (Saffredent).   [11] XIII (Saffredent).   [12] XXVI (Hircan).

Secret guilt is the worst kind.[13]

The servile attitude of the courtly lover turns into something quite different when he is alone with his beloved.[14]

A chaste lover is either a fool or *impuissant*.[15]

If women were actually as reluctant as they pretend to be, their wooers would have no recourse except trickery and violence.[16]

"The Italian maintains that the greater the sin, the greater the pleasure."[17]

"It is very difficult to repent of a thing that gives such pleasure...I have often confessed, but hardly repented it."[18]

"Deep love is very rare in women."[19]

"Women know neither love nor regret."[20]

"I have heard that the best of them like to have three [lovers]—one for honor, one for interest and the third for pleasure...but the first two serve the last."[21]

"When that sort of goods is for sale, they are always carried off by the highest and last bidder. Do not imagine that those who serve ladies take such a world of trouble for their sakes...It is for...their own pleasure."[22]

Enduring love is an impossibility.[23]

There is something to be said for the lady who prefers the attentions of a well-fed groom in good condition to those of a gentleman who has followed the army all his life.[24]

Thirty is the age when women give up trying to be considered beautiful in the hope of being considered wise.[25]

---

[13] xxi (Hircan). [14] x (Saffredent). [15] xviii (Simontault and Saffredent).
[16] xiv (Hircan). [17] xxxix (Simontault). [18] xxvi (Hircan).
[19] xlix (Hircan). [20] xxxii (Simontault). [21] liii (Saffredent).
[22] xiv (Geburon). [23] xviii (Geburon). [24] xx (Hircan).
[25] xxxv (Hircan).

Even the ladies are occasionally drawn into this practical train of thought, as when Longarine maintains that hypocrisy is very useful for hiding defects in virtue[26] and Parlamente herself explains why patience is "*une belle vertu*" — but not for wives[27] — and demonstrates the exact obligations involved in the term "*mercy*."[28] Nevertheless, although they do not present a completely united front (for Parlamente maintains a middle position between the rigidity of Oisille and the vacillations of the younger ladies) they are firm in their defence of a way of life which imposes some order and beauty upon the welter of human desires. The difficulty, as the men cynically point out, lies in the fact that for the realist all the conventions of courtly love are an illusion; the masking of desire results in hypocrisy and corruption, which rob the natural appetite of all its zest. Dagoucin, the unfulfilled Platonic lover, and Oisille, armed with her Scripture lessons, have one answer for this—asceticism. This alternative, however, is even less popular in the world of the *Heptameron* than it was in Boccaccio's domain. Longarine, Ennasuite and Nomerfide will go whichever way the wind blows; under Parlamente's leadership they hold out for etiquette and virtue, but their temperaments are scarcely more idealistic than those of the men—as the latter take wicked pleasure in pointing out.

Parlamente, however, possesses within herself twofold means for redeeming the squalor of human existence without withdrawing from society or abating a whit of its rightful pleasures. She is a romanticist, steeped in the religion of love and delighting in ceremony, panoply and all the drama of human passion; she is at the same time as realistic as anyone in the company. Since to be disillusioned without forfeiting the reality of one's dreams is a state which is unattainable in either of the old modes of experience, we must look into the Platonic reaches of Parlamente's spirit to discover its secret. By examining significant passages in the tales and conversations we may see that the medieval cult of love, anatomized ruthlessly by the men, reduced to cinders and re-placed by primitive desire, has in the mind of Hircan's wife become a kind of phoenix; it arises from those very ashes to prove that it is not only physically real but glorious and immortal. *L'amour*, partaking of

[26] LII.   [27] XXXVII.   [28] LVI.

68

the nature of both body and spirit, animates every rung of the ladder eloquently described in the nineteenth nouvelle and constitutes the sovereign power of the universe. This connects in many ways with liberal Christian doctrine, but Parlamente (who is not quite all of Marguerite) is for the most part more concerned with the resurrection of that cremated bird, love—now both sacred and profane.

The possibilities of these documentary tales are now multiplied two or three times, as the author demonstrates competently in the discussions. The question thus arises: would a more creative mind than hers have been able to restore depth and value to the situations by means of literary artistry alone? Or had the comprehensive viewpoint required for such a task become an impossibility in this century in France, ridden with doubts and nourished on a paradoxical concept of human nature? Marguerite, in her serene religious way, is just as difficult to pin down as her irreligious model. The frank sensual gusto which enlivens the remarks of Hircan and Simontault issues from the same nature which is tuned in its upper reaches to the most delicate spiritual nuances, but which is reluctant, nevertheless, to relinquish one for the other. The Queen is so much aware of this paradox that she projects it by means of Saffredent, who presents a playfully satiric argument: man gaily ascends the Platonic ladder by means of one erotic adventure after another—and it can all be proved by Scripture. *"Comment aymerez-vous Dieu, que vous ne voyez point, si vous n'aymez celluy que vous voyez?"*[29]

A narrative artist to whom truth seems to possess many faces must try for the next most stable thing—reality, as it is experienced through the senses, the activities and relationships of human beings. In the *Heptameron* Marguerite functions as a *raconteuse*, not as a creator. She does not attempt to transform the stories which she has collected, nor is there any reason why she should be expected to; her purpose is to entertain. Nevertheless, she cannot resist the urge to edify; she interpolates and prods when the action goes slack, instead of increasing the pace, and supplies motives from her private source to any character in need. Lovers in her tales who are obviously concerned with nothing but their private satisfactions must be made eligible for heaven; she gets them in by a

[29] XXXVI.

new ruling which has apparently been made since Paolo and Francesca took their places in the Second Circle: *"la porte de paradis n'est poinct refusée aux vraiz amans."* The Platonic lady of Pampeluna who expounds it in the twenty-sixth nouvelle also adds the assurance that they need not worry about Purgatory, either, since they suffer enough on earth—and proceeds to die forthwith. What has killed her is her virtue, victorious over desire—and no one could be happier than the ageing Oisille to see her perish. Parlamente solemnly expounds the place of reason in this catastrophe, but for once her remarks carry no weight. Saffredent, the teller of the tale, has just demonstrated by the most subtle irony that it makes no sense.

Fortunately, few of the nouvelles are as ridden with virtue as this one, but many contain lovers who are fully as long-winded as the lady of Pampeluna. Rhetorical habits which were formerly confined to characters in the exempla have now been ascribed to lusty young folk in their teens who would normally be given no chance to talk, but only a simple choice: making love, getting killed, or retiring to a monastery. It is particularly ironic when, as often happens, the verbose lover finally goes off and forgets the object of his affections, as does Rolandine's handsome bastard in the twenty-first nouvelle, or, like Amadour in the tenth, turns into a determined rapist in the twinkling of an eye. It is small wonder that Floride cries, *"Helas! Amadour, sont-ce icy les vertueux propos que durant ma jeunesse m'avez tenuz? Es-ce cy l'honneur et la conscience que vous m'avez maintesfoys conseillé plustost mourir que de perdre mon ame?"*

The truth of the matter is that for nearly four centuries the ideal of courtly love had flamed with all the intensity of a forbidden passion, filling the hearts of its knights with excitement and hope and concentrating their energies with remarkable effect. By the time it reached Floride and Amadour,[30] however, the code had subtly changed—for strong-minded ladies, if not for the men; morality was entering into it, which resulted in masculine desperation, feminine shock and mutual

---

[30] The Queen is apparently relating personal experience in this tale. Putnam, p. 58. *Bibliophiles Français*, quoted in Kelly, p. 80.

disillusionment. Poor Floride's personal lament forms the epitaph of a vanished age.

We are watching in the *Heptameron*, therefore, the disintegration of *amour courtois* and the uncertain formation of a new ideal appearing in its place. There are a number of examples of the *grande passion manquée* in addition to those cited: In the fifteenth nouvelle the lover is not troubled by any excess of chastity in his lady, but he goes away for too long and she forgets him. One frustrated pair do the best they can to sustain the tradition by becoming monk and nun, but they indulge in so much fainting and weeping in public before the final farewell that they appear to be destined for the infirmary rather than the chapel.[31] A distracted lover who is doomed to seven years of waiting becomes a hermit for good; the divine love which replaces human passion does not, however, prevent his returning to thumb his nose figuratively at the lady.[32] Still another reject refuses to come out of his monastery in spite of the fact that his luck turns.[33] Parlamente's spouse clarifies the situation here; he would have come fast enough, says Hircan, if she had not insisted upon matrimony.

The whole question of marriage comes up for review in these tales, since adultery can no longer be taken for granted by lovers in the old carefree way. Parlamente, for instance, states unequivocally that it is worse than death,[34] which makes matters exceedingly complicated in a society which regards marriage as a matter of title and property. Dagoucin speaks out against this kind of arrangement at the end of the fortieth nouvelle, and Geburon counters with more conservative views on the "indiscreet" unions based on love. Parlamente sets forth an impossible ideal—complete submission to God and a love-match sanctioned by both families—whereupon the four practical men all swear that this was exactly how their marriages began. Even if the author herself did not lift a quizzical eyebrow here, the reader would take their statement with a grain of salt, and Parlamente's pretty ideal, too—for without connubial mishaps there would certainly be few tales for the *Heptameron*. All of the ladies have obviously been inoculated with the new concept, for Longarine recites one of its chief tenets at the end of Nouvelle

[31] Nouvelle IX [32] XXXIV. [33] LXIV. [34] XXXII.

Sixty-Nine: "A chaste wife, who loves truly, finds more contentment in being loved than in all the pleasures which the flesh can desire."

This precept, to which Dagoucin, of course, subscribes completely, adds one large qualification to the medieval injunction that a wife must be subject to her husband; it is the obligation of "perfect" love which now devolves upon the husband as well as the wife. If this Platonic detail could be arranged, the effect of Longarine's pronouncement would be as thoroughgoing as the marriage regulations of the Church, and would sound the death-knell of *amour courtois*.

Parlamente, in giving voice to the beautiful paean to love which she shares with Longarine at the end of the nineteenth nouvelle is striving to restore to human passion the vitality lost through centuries of subterfuge and artificial convention and to demonstrate the power of sublimation known to religious mystics of all times. The restorative effect of innocence and the ideal is what she seeks. Still, when she says that "a heart that is virtuous towards God and man loves with more passion than a vicious heart, because the former is not afraid that the real nature of its sentiments should be apparent"[35] she is expressing an aspect of the psychological truth which Geburon approaches from the other direction. He extols the hearty, natural pleasures of "*les gens simples*"; her system depends upon refinement of mind and soul. "Is it not strange," she inquires with sublime snobbery, "that so fine a passion can enter such vulgar hearts?"[36]

Parlamente on her cloudy ladder and the forthright men planted solidly on the earth are actually more unified in their aims than the lady can admit, but the authoress whose mind she speaks is not confined to one character; she can also get at the truth through Geburon and the common sense of Hircan. In the meantime, everyone at Notre Dame de Serrance participates in the formal observances of the Church. Bells sound punctually for devotions, but sometimes they must ring and ring again. On the first day, vespers are delayed for more than an hour, out of courtesy to the guests, who have been engrossed in Parlamente's longest tale. On the second, the monks themselves are late; they have been stealthily listening to the story of the lady in the arms of her groom.

[35] Nouvelle XL   [36] XXIX.

This picture of monachal life follows the comic medieval pattern and the polite negligence of the company is Boccaccian—but there is another element here which has not appeared in any of the collections of tales considered so far. It is seen first in the morning Scripture readings of Oisille, which so captivate her friends that they are late for mass. Still, within the frame of the *Heptameron*, the stirrings of Reform are expressed in a lightly humorous vein. What happens in the tales themselves is a different matter entirely. Here the clergy are seen to be corrupt in all the old familiar ways, but the raucous medieval laughter is no longer forthcoming. These are no merry tales, but serious and often terrible indictments. The horrid prior of the twenty-second nouvelle is taken from life; it is impossible to read the realistic details and pay no heed to the cry of sœur Marie, which constitutes Marguerite's own message to the world: "...*Ce sont diables en lieu de religieux ceux qui nous viennent visiter!*"

The detested *Cordeliers* are the targets of most of Marguerite's sharpest barbs, for the Order of St. Francis has now deteriorated to the point where it is said to be "founded on the folly of women."[37] The regular clergy are not exempt, however; Oisille, at the end of the twenty-third nouvelle can not say anything good about them because everyone has agreed to tell the truth. The abuse of the Sacraments forms the basis for two tales (LI and XXX) and there is one sharp little anecdote dealing with false miracles and the profits to be made thereby.[38] The final nouvelle, in addition to its exposure of clerical corruption, also carries a minor mockery of the last rites; the monk and nun, before the seduction, are shouting "Jesus" into the dying man's ear. This satiric note is evident from time to time in the speech of Parlamente's friends, who merrily appropriate religious phrases and concepts for their own purposes. Thus Longarine, taunting Simontault concerning the perfect man, says "*et laudabimus eum,*" and Simontault himself, in another place, solemnly interprets the forty-first nouvelle as the effort of a monk to observe the Christmas spirit—by getting a young virgin with child.

Less innocent is the sound of Saffredent's *bon mot* near the end of the fifty-fourth tale. This would simply be a little word-play on the erotic

[37] Nouvelle XXXIV.   [38] LXV.

old verb *mourir*, except for his analogy. Oisille has been preaching about the duty of wives to serve their husbands as the Church serves Christ, and Parlamente is quick to bring her up to date with the remark, "Our husbands, madam, ought likewise to behave to us as Jesus Christ does to the Church." Emboldened by this sally, Saffredent goes her one better: "*Aussy faisons-nous, et, si possible estoit, nous le passerions, car Christ ne morut que une foys pour son Eglise; nous morons tous les jours pour noz femmes.*"

The lightness and verve which animate all of the discussions in the frame bear witness to Marguerite's keen sense of humor. The intellectual detachment upon which this depends, however, disappears with the launching of almost every tale. This is especially clear in the twenty-third, which in an older collection would have been treated as a fabliau exposing one more trick by which a lustful priest accomplishes his desires. Here it is treated as a document, stark and terrible, dogmatized by Oisille into a clearly Protestant exemplum.

The two categories in which the old tales naturally fell have become indistinguishable in the *Heptameron*. Everything that happens is purported to be *real*, and a good deal of the material is actually taken from life. Marguerite is no stranger to gross details; she is determined, however, to redeem them by applying the ideal as a kind of splint to all that she portrays—through demonstration, dialogue or comment from the region of the frame. Thus she feels no necessity for discrimination in the content of her tales, as long as they involve erotic stituations or some lively substitute in the way of violence, hardship, or (if Nouvelles xi and li are actually by her hand) sheer filth. Organization and balance are also unimportant to her; she applies these qualities where she likes, but not in her plots; a careful arrangement of the sequence of the stories[39] satisfies her need for order and the three-dimensional comments are intended to supply the rest.

When we remember that her primary purpose is to entertain (legend has it that the nouvelles were told to amuse her dying brother, Francis I)[40] and that she was also impelled by an almost medieval urge to edify, her

[39] Marguerite d'Angoulême, *L'Heptaméron*, ed. Michel François (Paris, 1960), p. xl.
[40] Putnam, p. 334.

74

achievement in reconciling these polarities is astonishing. For this reason she holds the highest place among story-tellers of her time and country,[41] whereas in poetry, where gifts of another order are required, she is surpassed by her protégés.[42]

Shorn of its external trappings, the picture of life which her nouvelles presents is curiously modern. It is ironic and absurd—for this is a cosmos ruled by an all-loving Creator who seems to have let things get seriously out of hand. The situation which is the source of Boccaccio's humor does not serve the Queen of Navarre so well. The atmosphere of most of the stories, underneath the incessant activity, is a kind of dreary *Angst*. This is especially noticeable in the long tales of Floride and Rolandine, where the lovers seem to be trying to live out romances, but succeed only in circling in a nervous round of complications. They are borrowed from life, but in presenting them their literary creator has used her mind rather than her senses and imagination. The ideals with which she equips them do not support their actions, and we cannot get close enough to them to know how they really feel. The author senses this, and piles on rhetorical reinforcements at every weak spot, but the characters remain unreal.

The true purpose of each nouvelle is accomplished after it is told, through the remarks of the commentators. Oisille moralizes everything, the men pull the action back to reality and Parlamente uses love to unify the scene. This works in a strange way when the whole point of a tale depends upon its immorality. In the Christmas fabliau, for instance, Simontault's gay impudence supplies the false analogy which makes the joke, but it comes post mortem; the story has already been impaled upon a pikestaff: "...The *Cordeliers* are so blind in their lust that they know neither fear nor prudence."

Marguerite's own explanation of humor may clarify her procedure somewhat, and may also explain the presence of the two stercoraceous items so difficult for modern minds to reconcile with the sensitivity of a poetess and a queen. Saffredent inquires after the end of the fifty-second nouvelle why women laugh at things which they protest are offensive to them; with admirable psychological insight, Parlamente

[41] Adolphe Chenevière, *Bonaventure des Périers, sa vie, ses poésies* (Paris, 1866), p. 125.
[42] Ibid., p. 126.

replies, "*Toute personne est encline à rire ou quant elle veoit quelcun tresbucher, ou quant on dict quelque mot sans propos, comme souvent advient la langue fourche en parlant et faict dire ung mot pour l'autre, ce qui advient aux plus saiges et mieulx parlantes.*" This sudden juxtaposition of the proper and improper is indeed the foundation of humor on its lowest level, but Parlamente goes on to protest that no honorable woman will listen to the deliberately scabrous talk of evil-minded men. Simontault then inquires why women giggle behind their masks—a question which neither Parlamente nor Longarine can answer save with a defence of feminine hypocrisy when virtue fails.

Humor, in Marguerite's mind, is linked with morality, and thus any *inadvertent* indignity may be described—even the plight of the lady in the eleventh nouvelle, exposed in full view "*au pire estat que une femme se porroit monstrer.*"[43] Most of the merry old world of the fabliau, however, is doomed from the start. Its matter-of-fact code, the foundation of all nocturnal escapades, is replaced with another which creates far fewer cuckolds than frustrated lovers. The adventure in the fourth nouvelle, for instance, which concerns Marguerite herself (under a false title) and the amorous Admiral of France, renders that worthy ridiculous because, for all his *bonnet de nuict* and handy trap-door, he gets nothing but scratches. Hircan, who knows a good fabliau when he hears it, turns thumbs down on this one. Something is radically wrong when two women can get the better of a man.

He is absolutely right, but this is potentially a very funny tale in spite of its feminist viewpoint. The author has achieved detachment in this instance because, with virtue in control, she can relax and enjoy the comic deflation of the lover. Nevertheless, she is still more concerned with expatiating on the rewards of chastity. The intolerably long-winded old *dame d'honneur* should have been strangled early in the proceedings— and in this recommendation Hircan and the reader are at one.

We now reach a curious but unavoidable conclusion concerning the world of the *Heptameron*. The Life Force, which always carried off even the crassest of the old tales to brisk and ludicrous victory and could lift

[43] Gruget, however, proved to be more squeamish and suppressed it in his edition of 1559, after which time a substitution was used. *L'Heptaméron*, Note 263.

the romances to extraordinary heights through sublimation, is in constant danger here of being short-circuited. Hircan and his confrères are right —if lovers were actually as chaste as they must pretend to be according to the newfangled ideal, society would be turned upside-down. Marguerite, following the example of Boccaccio, presents a panorama of raw human passion—and even more strictly limited than his to a single kind. Thus each tale or anecdote carries within it a *raison d'être*, but the idealist in Marguerite is always at odds with the realist who selected the material; she cannot let it alone. What she takes away with one hand, however, she endeavors generously to restore with the other—and her inimitable frame brings the work to life.

Like Des Périers, the Queen of Navarre expresses the various aspects of her personality in completely different literary forms. Her whole range, from the mystical poetry down through the courtly lyrics and little allegorical dramas with which she diverted herself in her earlier period, is finally brought down to earth in the *Heptameron*. Sensing that her collection is limited in quality, and having no intention of allowing it to remain so, she attempts to enrich its contents by a process which is no more successful than the formulas ironically repeated by the Canon's Yeoman.

As for the casket in which she has left seventy-two of the hundred pieces which she intended to store away, that is quite a different matter. It is an unpretentious work of art fashioned with such skill out of realistic materials that the thoughtful reader can see the very result which she hoped to achieve with the coins. Using Parlamente and Dagoucin as mouthpieces for the mystic incantations, she has actually achieved a transmutation of quality here; it is the Queen's treasure-box which constitutes the treasure.

When we consider the living models for her story-tellers, this interpenetration of real and ideal becomes clear. Marguerite's mother, for instance, had failings which are not visible in Oisille—and yet that stubborn and sanctimonious matriarch, always a bit too much on the right side, is a delightfully realistic character. The real Dagoucin has been identified as Marguerite's spiritual adviser,[44] a courtier-churchman

[44] Putnam, p. 135. Critical opinion concerning the prototypes of these characters is not unanimous; only Oisille and Parlamente are unmistakable.

of the untrammelled Renaissance pattern; he was apparently no less loath to woo a Queen platonically than was Des Périers to court his abbess, but in the *Heptameron* he appears simply as the masculine counterpart of Parlamente. He has no intellectual rapport with the men and appears to be considerably weaker than the lady whom he adores, but he is eloquent, wistful and charming. There is no place for him in the real world, but he is a real human being nonetheless. Hircan is a bluff, likable fellow, lusty and humorous, with an admirable hatred of hypocrisy, but from what we know of Marguerite's husbands (either of which Hircan may be), his is a touched-up portrait like the rest. All are types, but their creator individualizes them with great skill, without recourse to physical detail. Everything is done through conversation. Still, we know that Longarine inclines toward plumpness, that Saffredent enjoys his wine, and that Nomerfide cannot resist boasting about her lovers.

It is Parlamente, of course, who spiritualizes the group. She works at it consistently and with confidence; her mind is calm and lucid, but it is her energy which transforms her little world. Marguerite has crystallized her own best qualities in this delightful lady, but has not robbed her of life. She moderates the proceedings with finesse, but sometimes gets trapped in arguments and is forced to extricate herself through sheer verve; occasionally she reveals an astonishingly earthy point of view when discussing the mores of the Court. This ceases to be a matter for surprise, however, when we discover through the tales of Floride and of Admiral de Bonnivet's nightcap the kind of atmosphere which customarily enveloped the Queen.

Not only was her environment a worldly one; in her early life it was comparatively crude and deficient both in learning and sophisticated grace. Castiglione notes that the French court in his time could boast nothing to match the polished urbanity of the Italians. To him, the young Francis (still "*monsignor d'Angolem*") appeared to be a hopeful possibility for making his countrymen as proficient in letters as they were in arms. He had everything, including *grandezza dell' animo*, which might conceivably grace the throne of France.[45] He also had a sister, but

---

[45] Baldassare Castiglione, *Il Libro del Cortegiano* (Milan, n.d.), p. 72. Reference noted in Putnam, p. 34.

the importance of this asset was yet to be fully demonstrated. In retrospect, all critics are unanimous in noting the revival of the chivalric ideal during the reign of Francis I, and in paying tribute to the refining and civilizing influence of Marguerite, who combined *"la gaieté gauloise de ses ancêtres et le raffinement de ses modèles italiens, la ferveur humaniste de la Renaissance et la ferveur mystique de la Réforme."*[46] During her brother's reign, Marguerite (along with her mother, while she lived) exerted a powerful influence over this handsome, pleasure-loving king; through her personal enthusiasms and gifted protégés she extended this influence to the arts and letters of her time. Thus the Renaissance was ushered into France under feminine auspices; the place of woman in this new and challenging world was a vital matter to Marguerite, and this concern is reflected throughout the *Heptameron*, giving it a tone and point of view quite different from that of other collections. Putnam (paraphrasing M. Lanson) describes the change dramatically: "She broke the line which runs from the fabliaux to Voltaire; she made the *conte* a method for the notation and description of human passions."[47]

Stated thus, her contribution to the genre appears more weighty—and less so—than she meant it to be. She began with paradoxical intent: to entertain her hearers richly and scandalously and to elevate their souls. To salvage even an ambiguous ideal from the midst of her realistic scenes she found it necessary to discuss and to declaim. With this surrender of detachment—an essential ingredient of the exemplum, the fabliau and even the romance—Marguerite signed the death-warrant of the medieval tale.

Her great gift to the literature of her time, however, extends beyond the confines of a single form. The *Heptameron* presents variations on old themes, but her neoplatonic poetry is a message from another world— the first of its kind to appear in France. Not only the ideas but "...*le vocabulaire et le style, les comparaisons et les images...tout ici est nouveau."*[48] Here the ancient Greek idealism which had reappeared across the Pyrenees assumes a new reality and a new tongue. Reanimating and

[46] P. Castex & P. Surer, *XVIe Siècle* (Paris, 1946), p. 6.
[47] Putnam, p. 337.
[48] Lefranc, p. 214.

syncretizing, it offers promise of a grand reconciliation of opposites— faith and reason, reform and reaction, Christian charity and *amour courtois*. Through the pages of the *Heptameron* it struggles valiantly, trapped in an atmosphere in which it cannot subsist; but in one matchless passage at the end of the nineteenth nouvelle, "*l'un des plus elévés que la Renaissance française nous ait transmis,*"[49] it remains forever enshrined in words:

"*J'appelle parfaictz amans…ceulx qui cherchent, en ce qu'ilz aiment, quelque parfection, soit beaulté, bonté ou bonne grace; tousjours tendans à la vertu…car l'ame, qui n'est creée que pour retourner à son souverain bien, ne faict tant qu'elle est dedans ce corps, que desirer d'y parvenir….*"

---

[49] Lefranc, pp. 246-7, 209.

CHAPTER SIX

THE KALEIDOSCOPIC WORLD OF BANDELLO

At the same time that the Queen of Navarre and her *valet de chambre* were composing their nouvelles, another collection destined for literary fame was taking shape in Italy under the hand of Matteo Bandello. This urbane Dominican, whose life amid the courts and *salotti* is reflected in great detail in his stories, paid tribute to *"la cristianissima prencipessa"* in his dedication of one novella[1] and perhaps, in a more subtle way, by appropriating a number of her tales. The evidence of such confiscation, however, is not clear. It is impossible to discover exactly which writer borrowed from the other or whether they made use of common sources,[2] since Bandello, like Marguerite, used materials that came to him in a number of different ways. Thus his critics are divided into two camps: the accusers, led by Di Francia, who charge him with plagiarism and brazen distortions of the truth concerning his sources, and the defenders, including Brognoligo and Manginelli.[3]

For our purposes, however, it is less important to take sides concerning the probity of this novelliere than to measure his success in creating that atmosphere of reality which is so important to him. He is noteworthy not only for the sheer bulk of his two hundred and fourteen novelle,

[1] Matteo Bandello, *Tutte le opere*, a cura di Francesco Flora (Verona, 1952), II, Part IV, Novella 19.

[2] Ibid., I, II: Notes on Part I: 9, 11, 16, 39; Part II: 24; Part IV: 10. Flora points out similarities between these tales and six in the *Heptameron* but draws no conclusions.

[3] Ibid., I, 114-115. Gwynfor Griffith, *Bandello's Fiction* (Oxford, 1955), p. 138. Griffith also surveys the controversy and makes measured judgment here.

but for the manner in which they mirror *"vivissimamenti i costumi e le passioni quotidiane dell'etá sua."*[4] Scholars have demonstrated that his tendency in adaptation is to supply verisimilitude and good psychological detail, to play up dramatic scenes and to write in the long melodramatic speeches which pleased the taste of his time.[5] In addition, he makes use of a typical courtly device—the dedicatory letter to a person of position and influence. Every tale, from the fifty-three-page history to the most superficial anecdote, is provided with its obsequious epistle. These dedications are so interwoven with real, half-real and perhaps wholly fictional events that every Bandello scholar has become hopelessly bogged down in them. Some letters have apparently been added after the stories were written; some seem to have been taken from one tale and applied to another; a few appear to have been solemnly dedicated to persons already dead and gone. However, the verisimilitude thus achieved is remarkable in its own right. One need only to recall the marvellously systematic fabrications of Defoe and Swift to recognize a kindred journalistic spirit here.

It is clear that Bandello is not so much concerned with the edification of his readers as he is with their pleasure. Griffith, from the author's preface and the dedication to the twenty-fourth novella in Part II has pieced together the statement that his "own declared alms were to please and to set down those things that might prove to be instructive precedents."[6] The two are not necessarily opposed. So paradoxical is the human spirit that it can be delighted with that which ennobles as well as with that which debases, and sometimes with both at once—and if ever this gloriously ambiguous characteristic was seen in an age, that age was the Cinquecento. Bandello, the worldly cleric, can preach and moralize with utter seriousness upon occasion, but those occasions are rare; they contribute a comfortable air of sanction to the ribald entertainment, and serve to illustrate an aspect of contemporary life.

However, for the most part, Bandello's countrymen in *"quel tempo fervido e coltissimo, avventuroso e crudele"*[7] recognized reality only in the form of direct physical experience. More exalted concepts, which in

---

[4] Bandello, I, xii.   [5] Griffith, p. 8.
[6] Griffith, p. 124.   [7] Bandello, I, xi.

the fourteenth century were becoming ambiguous, had by the sixteenth disappeared in a vast spiritual "negation" whose fruits were profligacy and indifference. In that age, in which a quixotic and bloodthirsty *onore* was substituted for morals, when the clergy, especially those of the mendicant orders, were hated and ridiculed as a matter of course, and sexual license was so common that it required special features of degradation or cruelty to arouse interest, it is remarkable that the novelle could nevertheless reflect some gentler modes of life. A courtly existence, privileged, urbane, intellectually free, admirable and charming on the surface, is portrayed in the pages of the more competent literary men. Burckhardt notes the civilizing value of this kind of writing, and states that France learned arts of refinement and grace through the imitation of precisely such ambassadors of *savoir faire* as Matteo Bandello.[8] Nevertheless, a more profound reality, harsh, bestial and violent, was always lurking beneath the polished surface, ready at any moment to spring forth and assume control of human life.

Love and death (usually in their more primitive forms of lust and murder) are the themes which dominate Bandello's tales. Although Rotunda has isolated fourteen others, and Petrocchi boils them all down to *amore*,[9] it is clear that this novelliere is partial to two—and with good reason. They are ancient, universal and gripping, and may be presented in many forms, from jest to tragedy. Best of all, for his purposes, is the effect when they are transmitted as glorified gossip—and such material, to be savory, must be rich in physical detail. Here Bandello provides generously: the quick gush of blood, the sound of chattering teeth, the odor of carrion and sudden attack of nausea, the flicker of candles held high over a bed at midnight—all are described with vivid effect. Even the classic story of Lucrezia's rape, for all its high-flown dialogue, contains an intimate feminine confession: the lady, who is only "*donna di carne come l'altre*," found the experience not totally unpleasant.

In a sensual age, among hot-blooded people, there appears to be little

[8] Jacob Burckhardt, *The Civilization of the Renaissance in Italy*, trans. S. Middlemore (New York and London, 1929), p. 199.
[9] Griffith, p. 21 (note).

use in trying to hide the truth or to avoid naming acts which are not supposed to be subjects for polite conversation. Bandello's real world is a mélange of villainous priests, cuckolded husbands, rape, castration, feigned and hidden pregnancies, incest, abortion, impotence and perversion. In their train, in myriad brutal and shocking forms, there often follows mutilation or death. Still, much of this is intended to be taken lightly. Given the fabliau convention that no one after dark ever recognizes his or her bedfellow (which is relinquished here occasionally, as in the story of the amorous Losco brothers, just for fun) this author makes full use of all the comic appurtenances such as rope ladders, chimneys, covered chests, bribes, disguises and lies. Since anything becomes dull through repetition, the only way to sustain interest in a series of similar escapades is to select the unusual twist, the grotesque or sickening punishment, or the fiendish revenge which will carry the reader on to the next page and the next novella.

Bandello also obliges his readers by being very explicit. Everything is called by its common name or familiar slang term, except for those acts or functions which become more ludicrous through euphemism, like "*mandare a Corneto*" (repeated ad infinitum), "*fare la congiunzione dei pianeti*" and the courtly "*tributo a la contessa di Laterino.*" Sins against nature are treated casually, and in a mocking tone. Porcellio maintains naively that they are not unnatural for *him*, thus confounding his holy confessor.[10] When the ladies are out of the way, Bandello seizes the occasion to carry out this theme more fully with a series of scandalous anecdotes about the notorious Mantuan archdeacon, couched in current terms including the stock-phrase "*carne di capretto.*"[11]

Thus, although the reader is not able to remember many of the characters individually, he experiences with extraordinary immediacy what most of them do, and how they react to the conditions of their lives. He learns that matrimony in this matter-of-fact world is necessary yet almost always insupportable; that any young woman, maid or wife, is fair game for any clever man, of whatever station; that most husbands are cuckolds; that virginity commonly melts like snow after the age of

[10] Bandello, Part I, Novella 6.
[11] I, 30.

84

twelve, and chastity is so rare as to merit a novella and a monument.[12] Husbands are within their rights when they kill and dismember their wives' lovers—if they can catch them; monasteries are invariably sources of corruption. Everyone knows (except some young brides whose instruction has been sadly neglected)[13] what makes a lady *gravida*—but it is a rare girl indeed who ever worries about it, before marriage or afterwards.

This seems like the medieval world bereft of its religious upper story, and, as in the tales of Marguerite of Navarre, curiously deficient also in the abode of courtesy which belongs in the middle. A transformation commonly occurs in the Italian atmosphere of the court after the candles are blown out: the *palazzo* itself becomes the tricky, bestial realm of the fabliau.

Still there remain within these tales some serene and irrational remnants of two great ideals for which human beings may live and die—*cortesia*, with all of its obligations in the name of honor, and the spiritual reality represented by the Church. There is also a third entity which can be seen springing up oddly from three separate sources, and which finally assumes almost complete independence. This is the ideal of chastity, a "sacred" virtue in the tales of classical origin, and which reveals neoplatonic implications in the new versions. When it is demonstrated in Bandello's contemporary world, *castità* sometimes stems dimly from Christian teaching, but finds itself so much at odds with its environment that the consequences are wildly dramatic.

The tales which are infused strongly with any of these three ideals are rare in Bandello's collection, but those in the first category are the most numerous, and all of the dedicatory letters emanate an almost tangible atmosphere of elegance and grace. "*L'onore, cui senza né donna né uomo deverebbe restar in vita*" makes extravagant claims upon its noble devotees, who, although they may appear as exotic foreigners, demonstrate *magnificenzia, liberalità* and *magnifica gratitudine* with unmistakably Latin flourishes.[14] The Queen of Hungary is a good example; this "*cortesissima reina*" knows a real gentleman when she sees one; her favorite displays

[12] I, 8.   [13] III, 3.
[14] I: 2, 45, 49; II: 15, 16, 26, 52.

the requisite *"valore e generosità de l'animo e l'altre mille belle parti"* and is richly rewarded with material benefits.[15] Other courtly lovers suffer heroically for their inamoratas, like Don Diego in his grotto,[16] but not all are as fortunate in the end as he; Filiberto remains speechless for three years for a kiss, but finally runs out of patience,[17] and Carlo and his secret beloved[18] suffer deaths almost as dramatic as those of the celebrated Romeo and Giulietta.[19]

These ideal and sacrificial loves, which outweigh everything in the cosmos for the participants, stand out vividly in the lecherous Bandellian world. The author dramatizes the situation in each case, sometimes achieving a considerable amount of intensity and sometimes drowning the affair in floods of self-conscious dialogue. Still, it is clear that these tales have been selected primarily for their melodramatic accessories — jealousy, anguish and bloodshed; the *grande passion* itself is a secondary dividend.

Religion, however, is a matter which requires of the literary Bishop of Agen a direct approach. There are four separate choices available to him as he mirrors the spiritual values of his world, and he calmly takes all of them. The first is to ignore the possibility of a deity, and to concentrate upon human action, ruled by chance. The second is to portray an amoral humanity ridden by corrupt priests. The third is to expose Catholic superstitions and clerical hypocrisy in the interest of an enlightened faith, and the last is to accept the Church with childlike simplicity, superstitions and all.

The last two appear to possess latent power to redeem Bandello's world, if he were interested in such matters. However, he remains totally absorbed in his task of recounting events, and here he is aided by a keen eye and an excellent ear. He is remarkably fluent in his mimicry of priestly dialogues and exhortations, especially when they are used for derision—for example, the futile speeches of Porcellio's confessor,[20] Fra Bernardino da Feltro[21], and the pacifist preacher who, instead of the word *"pace,"* calls forth from his witless follower an unexpected obscenity.[22]

[15] I, 45.   [16] I, 27.   [17] III, 7.
[18] IV, 5.   [19] II, 9.   [20] I, 6.
[21] III, 10.   [22] III, 49.

This is by no means the kind of mockery which is intended to expose evil; it is simply a sophisticated secular jibe at the cleric who mouths words and communicates nothing.

When the exhortations concern a real abuse, however, Bandello's attitude becomes more complicated, for he combines his secular disillusion with the authority of the orthodox priest. His gay account of Fra Bernardino's humiliation is both an anticlerical joke and a theological rebuke, since the Franciscan's exaltation of his patron saint borders absurdly on hyperdulia. The general habit of scoffing thus appears to acquire official sanction. This negative emphasis is well exemplified in the story of the priest called "Borsello," who demolishes the popular cult of St. Francis' cord by fabricating an ingenious counter-superstition.[23] The way is thus officially left open for something more uplifting —"*l'opere de la carità*" and the "*comandamenti di Cristo*"—but these vague benefits are overshadowed by the unstated conclusion to which the tale inevitably leads: even the best of priests are shameless liars.

Nevertheless, the realm from which true miracles come is not completely closed to Bandello's readers. If they like, they may believe in his version of a symbolic baptismal miracle in the tradition of the old exempla,[24] the harsh retribution which fell upon two schismatic prelates in Poitiers,[25] or the amiable behavior of the lions which were expected to devour a lady falsely accused. The author notes confidently in this tale that "*l'innocenzia sempre è da Dio aiutata.*"[26] However, since the circumstances recounted in all the rest of the two hundred and fourteen novelle combine solidly to refute any such possibilities, the miracles serve more for literary contrast than for assurance. Amid innumerable descriptions of violent death it is refreshing to Bandello's "*candidi ed umani lettori*" to see one victim emerge unscathed—especially when the villain is at hand to furnish a meal for the lions.

Much more useful than supernatural assistance in the world of these novelle is the faculty for coming out with a clever quip at the right time. Making five virgins pregnant is a misdemeanor, but the guilty priest who relates it to the parable of the talents reduces his feat to a good joke

[23] III, 14.   [24] IV, 12.   [25] IV, 15.   [26] I, 24.

—obviously worth more than a few maidenheads any day.[27] Although Griffith points out that Bandello does not include all of the anticlerical material in his sources,[28] his censorship has obviously been liberal. Other satirical thrusts include a sharp jibe directed at the Carmelites (which exposes an undignified squabble for precedence among the mendicant orders)[29] and two other palpable hits—the ludicrous descriptions of the priest and bishop who try to exorcise, with all of the sacred paraphernalia at their command, a female monkey on the loose[30] and a little black *asino.*[31] The symbolic connotation of ass and monkey is thus wittily transferred to the prelates fearfully chanting their *Salve* and sprinkling holy water, without a superfluous word on the part of the author.

The sacraments, uses and traditions of the Church are never explicitly mocked by Bandello, but are almost always presented with journalistic accuracy in a setting which renders them ridiculous. Occasionally they are taken as a matter of course and then lost in the shuffle of external events. Pandora commits a frightful infanticide. Baptism does not occur to her, but for the author-priest who tells the tale, the deed begins to take on a more profound moral implication which he instantly negates by pulling the reader back to the world of matter, where Pandora is calling the hungry mastiff.[32]

The habit of keeping the reader stunned but earthbound is not un-conscious in Bandello; it is the result of his creed as a novelliere. To him, the art of story-telling lies in describing unusual happenings in everyday life, especially those which "*inducono a meraviglia,*"[33] but this wonder has nothing to do with the human imagination or spirit. De Sanctis, who sees the novella of the Cinquecento as "the *Decameron* in putrefaction,"[34] notes the change of taste which became evident after two centuries: a decline from courtly elegance and refinement to the "curiosity, buf-foonery, sensuality" of the bourgeoisie. The deftly ambiguous relation-ship which Boccaccio had maintained with the world of supernatural grace was lost as religion in Italy "expired in laughter, irony and license."[35]

[27] III, 56. [28] Griffith, p. 117. [29] III, 32. [30] III, 65.
[31] III, 44. [32] III, 52. [33] I, 51, noted in Flora's preface, Vol. I, xiv.
[34] Francesco De Sanctis, *History of Italian Literature*, trans. Joan Redfern (New York, 1931), I, 459.
[35] John A. Symonds, *The Renaissance in Italy* (New York, 1887), II, 494.

The clergy, like the suave and prolific Bandello, often turned their education and rich experience to secular ends and revealed themselves as the most satiric and scandalous story-tellers of them all. Burckhardt speculates as to the reason for this: Was it because in their privileged positions they "ran no risk" of ecclesiastical retribution? Were they attempting to exonerate themselves by exposing the follies of their fellow-clerics? Both of these suppositions are so paradoxical that they defy logical answers. Burckhardt's third suggestion, however, seems to be the most likely: the novellieri in holy orders simply reflected their own "selfish pessimism."[36]

Whatever the true attitude of Bandello the Dominican may have been, his well-stocked collection, when considered as a treasure-trove, is quite different from any of those discussed so far. For one thing, it appears in an unusual container—no carefully-wrought casket, but a sort of mailbag stuffed with letters, each of which contains a single coin. Also, in addition to its marked increase in quantity, the whole thing boasts a comprehensiveness lacking in Des Périers' bright currency and a unity which Marguerite, for all her ingenuity, could not achieve.[37] Since it has been demonstrated to contain a measure of the fine metal of idealism (borrowed, it is true, but nonetheless present in the tales) in addition to the crasser material which forms the bulk of its coinage, it should theoretically be sound enough to purchase a world which, like that of Chaucer, is organically whole yet dual in nature. However, this is obviously not the case; the Bandellian cosmos, obtainable at the price of those two hundred and fourteen assorted coins, rests on a single plane. The borrowed pieces, then, for all their original value, have gone for naught; their collector has set no store by them because to him their value is merely historic or theatrical. Mingled with the common coins they tend to lose their unearthly color and sheen and are no longer negotiable in their original categories. To restore them it would be necessary to remove them bodily from Bandello's sack. In the meantime, they

[36] Burckhardt, p. 244.
[37] Every element in Bandello's manifold world is contained within his tales. His Platonic love poetry and Petrarchistic verses are polite literary exercises rather than expressions of a deeper or more refined side of his nature.

remain, imparting to the whole collection a quality which is neither homogeneous nor heterogeneous, yet nothing like the graceful ambiguity of Boccaccio. Whereas the Tuscan always confines his contradictory values within a single tale at a time, the Lombard provides straightforward novelle and mixes his *types* without discrimination. The result is what Berard de Gerald, in a rhyming preface to Boaistuau's French adaptations, calls "*un grand Chaos d'ouvrage.*"[38] The necessity for maintaining variety in a multitude of similar situations leads inevitably to realism and then to sensationalism—the surest means in Bandello's power to evoke the gasp, the shudder, the wink and the sudden loud guffaw.

In accordance with this journalistic credo he frankly ignores formal rules of rhetoric, except in the long speeches and trumpeting dedications. His dialect, he confesses, is "*rozza e zotica lingua*" compared with the more literary Tuscan, but "...*cotesta sorte di novelle possa dilettare in qualunque lingua ella sia scritta.*"[39] His ordinary choice is prosaic, factual, but often vividly descriptive language. Although Di Francia notes that he usually presents his material in a more verbose style than that of his sources,[40] Bandello's decorations are not applied everywhere, and certainly never without a practical reason. When he waxes florid, it is to please a patron or to salvage a weltering plot. Lucrezia's rape, for instance, is carried out much too speedily for his purposes.[41] Something must obviously be done to extend the titillations of this climax, even in retrospect—and so the lady is given seven pages of talk. Her syntax, under the circumstances, is remarkable:

"... *Quello che io con altrui testimonio provar non posso e che non conviene che con le mie sole parole testifichi, col mio sangue farò certo, ed apertamente dimostrero non qual si sia morte essermi stata di spavento cagione, ma solo aver temuto la privazione de l'onore, cui senza né donna né uomo deverebbe restar in vita, perciò che perduto che è l'onore, nulla di buono a la persona resta....*"

The two lovers of Borgogni display similar talents when their "*lungo,*

[38] Bandello, I, xxxix.
[39] Ibid., "*Il Bandello ai Candidi ed Umani Lettori,*" p. 4.
[40] Griffith, p. 11.   [41] II, 21.

fortunato e segreto amore" is betrayed.[42] Since there is nothing left for them to do except perish—a commonplace ending in Bandello's world—the author makes up the deficit with literary anguish. Hysterical Cinzia, too, who believes that she has poisoned herself, inflates the silly situation with unflagging rhetoric.[43]

The pompous eloquence of Fra Bernardino da Feltro, however, turns a minor anecdote into a clever satire. In this case the flow of words is comic; the whole point is the humiliation of the speaker. In longer and weaker stories Bandello often attempts to inject vitality through dialogue which actually negates his desired effect. A more skilful writer might carry off this expedient successfully; one more gifted would not require it. However, the artificial harangues which he enjoys did not affect his contemporaries as they do the modern reader. Combined with his scenes of violent death, they reflected the temper of the time and created a new atmosphere in the novella—that of tragedy.[44] The uninhibited flow of blood and rant, catalyzed by Bandello's concrete knowledge of human frailty, turned many of his tales into miniature dramas in essence, awaiting the touch of a master to bring them to artistic life. Shakespeare's *Romeo and Juliet* and Webster's *The Tragedy of the Duchess of Malfi* were soon to realize the full artistic possibilities of the Bandellian matrix.

As for the creator of that matrix, he remained a stranger to the detachment which enables a literary genius to view his fellow-man with insight and compassion, and identified himself closely with the factual world which he depicts, by every means except that of emotion. What served him in lieu of artistic detachment was an impassivity which allowed him to move competently over the surface of life, feeling nothing but recording all.

This absence of tragic insight is closely related to his lack of genuine humor, and results from the same cause. Although a great number of his tales are intended to be comic, the modern reader, who still enjoys Boccaccio, fails to respond. Symonds demonstrates that the tendency to "tolerate, condone and compromise" in a society of unparalleled depravity accounts for the dearth of any great satire or comic writing during the Cinquecento. Lack of righteous anger and artistic imagina-

---

[42] IV, 5.   [43] II, 40.   [44] Bandello, I, xlviii.

tion had allowed the comic spirit to deteriorate into coarse glee which sniggered at the spectacle of vice. Both Symonds and De Sanctis deplore this "comic defect"; one of man's greatest gifts had "worn itself out by constant repetition and had sunk into being shameless and inartistic."[45]

It is this situation rather than a cultural gap which explains why we cannot laugh at Bandello's stories of the draper who stationed his apprentice in the conjugal bed[46] or the little bride who amputated the object which was disturbing her rest.[47] Even the tale which both Symonds and De Sanctis cite as one of his really humorous ones—the story of the monkey dressed in the clothing of a dead woman, who frightens a houseful of people out of their wits—is more macabre than genuinely comic. The author's chief concern is to show the solemn idiocy of the cleric who tries to exorcise the family pet, but the point loses its sharpness because of poor timing and the mass of vivid but extraneous detail. A better candidate for comic honors is the story of that lively Bigolino, whose ingenious and irrepressible *beffe* expose an avaricious bishop and win for the trickster a fine dinner besides.[48]

This light-hearted escapade is a startling contrast to the gratuitous coarseness and cruelty which so often appear as substitutes for humor in Bandello's tales; but we cannot be too critical. The author is not only one of the most prolific novellieri of his time, but one of the best. Symonds points out that the Lombard writers were romantically inclined, while the Tuscans (like Il Lasca) were more skilful at humor,[49] but Bandello's comic defect is not balanced by ardor; his love-stories are as matter-of-fact as all the rest. He is a recorder, not an interpreter. Where there are no standards it requires a genius to resurrect the spirit which lies beyond the facts of human life.

In this objective recording he demonstrates an exceptional skill in evoking reality through physical detail, as well as a broad knowledge of human psychology. It is not actual life which he puts down on paper, but the lively simulacrum which results when he applies to his materials the factual data gathered directly from experience in his contemporary world. The description of Giulia da Gazuola, quietly attiring her dishonored

[45] De Sanctis, p. 459.   [46] IV, 28.   [47] III, 3.
[48] III, 16.   [49] Symonds, p. 61.

young body in its finest array, and the shock of the little sister who is led to watch her drown are composed with fine economy and selective detail;[50] the effect here is remarkably like that achieved by some stories of de Maupassant. The horrors of Pandora's abortion are depicted with a kind of diabolical clarity; the native detachment of the writer in this case serves him well. As for Cinzia, who develops psychosomatic symptoms from drinking a glass of flavored water, her adolescent pangs and posturings are so knowingly set forth that she might well be included in a professional case-book.

This richly burgeoning realism is Bandello's greatest contribution to the novella—a verisimilitude which remains calmly independent of historical fact. Paradoxically, this lively new phenomenon springing up in an old form does not mark its perfection as an art; it is a subtle sign of decay. The devolution of man's fullest expression of himself—from religion to art to document[51]—is here demonstrated in its final stage. However, as a collector, a gaily inaccurate and vivid chronicler of actual events, Bandello overshadows all of his fellow novellieri of the Cinquecento and provides a kaleidoscopic reflection of the customs, manners and spirit of an age.[52]

---

[50] I, 8.
[51] Joseph Wood Krutch, *The Modern Temper* (New York, 1956), p. 97.
[52] Bandello, I, xii, xlviii.

CHAPTER SEVEN

BORROWED WORLDS: THE NOVELLA IN
SIXTEENTH-CENTURY ENGLAND

England was late in making the acquaintance of the Italian novella of
the Cinquecento, but responded with enthusiasm to the publication of
the first volume of William Painter's *Palace of Pleasure* in 1566. Roger
Ascham's famous diatribe directed against "fond books, of late translated
out of Italian into English, sold in every shop in London"[1] bore witness
not only to the sudden popularity of this collection,[2] but to Ascham's
perspicacity. It was perfectly clear to him that these stories, despite the
insistently moral wrappings in which they made their appearance,
reflected a cynical and licentious world—and he, as an upright and
strong-minded Englishman, wanted none of it.

Few of his compatriots shared his views, however, for Painter's borrowed "novells," like the "discourses" of Geoffrey Fenton, appeared in
English masquerading as exempla. All of the lurid Italian details were
there, but were now respectably hedged in with militant Christian
precepts. This ambiguous state of affairs must be blamed upon Boaistuau
and Belleforest, the diligent but uninspired French translators of a hundred and one *Histoires Tragiques*, most of which were taken from Bandello. Although the former translated only six tales, he passed on to his
successor a manner and style which were to exert a marked, though

[1] Roger Ascham, excerpt from *The Schoolmaster*, in Hyder and Rollins, eds., *The Renaissance
in England* (Boston, 1954), p. 833.
[2] Authorities differ as to the identity of these "books"; Pruvost believes that Ascham was
referring to Fenton's *Tragicall Discourses* as well as to Painter's *Palace*. René Pruvost, *Matteo
Bandello and Elizabethan Fiction* (Paris, 1937), p. 66.

temporary effect upon English prose.[3] While editing the *Heptameron*, Boaistuau had absorbed Marguerite's didactic method of transmitting the nouvelle, but not the wit and genuine spirituality with which she enlivened her collection. Belleforest, a mediocre literary hanger-on, possessed no more resources than he. What emerges in the *Histoires* is a series of Bandellian plots overlaid with moral harangues, discourses, anticlerical outbursts (almost Protestant in tone) and the complicated machinery of courtly love, rattllng along in awkward double yoke with holy matrimony. Bandello's natural appetite becomes a *"brutale passion"*[4] unredeemed by Marguerite's Platonism, and the feminist point of view which enlivens her *Heptameron* gives way to an attitude of Puritan harshness, masculine and uncompromising. Plots are altered to fit the adapter's will; rhetoric and classical allusions, complicated similes and passages of verse add a solemn and erudite tone—but underneath these impedimenta the fiery Italian bloodstream still courses—unregenerate and fascinating as ever.

It was this pseudo-classical French overlay upon Bandello which attracted William Painter, who used the French versions available to him and imitated their style even when translating directly from the Italian. Boccaccio, too, he admired for his "gravitie and sententious discourse," although he condemned some of his matter[5]—whereas Bandello's language he rejected summarily as "barren soile."[6] Nevertheless, the "tragicall Novells and dolorous Histories" which Painter selected from his store could make "profitable and pleasant reading" for Englishmen—with a little Frenchifying.

This process the book-loving Clerk of Her Majesty's Ordnance in the Tower carried out in various degrees in all of his translations, so that his thirty-three classical tales as well as the sixty-eight from French and Italian sources emerge in English all of a piece. He by no means succeeded in unifying by his borrowed method the values and realities of human

---

[3] Pruvost presents evidence to show that it was the French fondness for Amadis romances which influenced the style of these Gallic adaptations of Bandello and made its mark on Elizabethan prose through the English translators. Pruvost, pp. 6-7.

[4] Frank S. Hook, ed., *The French Bandello* (Columbia, Missouri, 1948), pp. 13-15.

[5] William Painter, *The Palace of Pleasure* (London, 1929), II, 8.

[6] Ibid., p. 9.

life, but he was the first Englishman to present to his countrymen the rich resources of the novella literature which had been circulating since the time of Chaucer in foreign tongues.[7]

In general, he was a faithful and accurate translator; it was not his aim to transform the tales, but to transmit them. When he adapted or moralized it was for literary reasons, and at such times he simply imitated the French. The whole façade of complacent English virtue which he sets up in his dedicatory letters to the Earl of Warwick and Sir George Howard is somewhat preposterous, considering that for years he was busily engaged in "ymbeseling" Her Majesty's powder, falsifying his accounts and piling up a comfortable fortune. An eminently practical man, he was well aware of the difference between human action and the conventions of society. The histrionic approach to the "novells" appealed to him, for it required no real discrimination; the most shocking vice could be dramatized into respectability. His translations thus became for him not only "a very court and palace" but "a stage and theatre for shew of true nobilitye, for profe of passing loialty and for tryal of their contraries" as well as a manual offering "rules for avoiding of vice and imitation of vertue to al estates."[8]

Painter has actually left little personal imprint upon his work, yet he has imparted to it an indefinably English stamp. He has accomplished this through his choices—selecting for the most part stories of action, bloodshed and adventure—and by his use of local terms and realistic detail. An examination of his treatment of a few typical tales will reveal some other tendencies:

His affinity for the masculine activity of the classical scene is shown in his use of Livy's version of the Lucrece story rather than that of Bandello (although he uses some of the latter as well).[9] Livy's tale is essentially political, and resounds with the clash of arms, as does that of Painter. Here the rape functions merely as the cause for vengeance, rebellion and battle. The outrage itself is dealt with summarily: "...His fleshlye and licentious enterprice overcame the puritie of her chaste and honest hart, which done he departed." The victim commits suicide and the

[7] Painter, I, xiii.   [8] Ibid., II, 8.
[9] Painter, Novella II; Bandello, Part II, 21.

vengeance proceeds. Bandello, as we have seen in the previous chapter, dwells upon her sensations and then upon the conflict between her sense of pollution and the ideal of chastity. Painter is quite capable of imitating this vein, but does not choose to do so when there is a rousing battle afoot. Most of his classical tales exemplify clearly but remotely, like images seen through the wrong end of a telescope, the old ideals of loyalty, generosity and courage.

His treatment of Boccaccio is less sure; it is conscientious but humorless. Lacking the Tuscan's sense of ambiguity, Painter sometimes reproduces a whole tale almost exactly but misses the point. The anecdote of the amorous old courtier who justifies his lust by a quip about leeks[10] is in the original an exercise in repartee, transparently disguised as a moral lesson. Painter solemnly takes Boccaccio at his word. In another light-hearted tale, Rinaldo (in the *Decameron*), stripped by thieves, prays to St. Julian and is forthwith supplied with food, shelter, a hot bath and a willing bed-companion.[11] This ironic demonstration of the efficacy of prayer appears in Painter in a totally different light. The complaisance of the "lecherous lady" is disposed of hastily, with apologies, and the full effect of the prayer is shifted to the punishment of the thieves and the restoration of Rinaldo's property.

Since the tone and style of the *Heptameron* are congenial to Painter, he renders sixteen of Marguerite's tales into English with little change except to boil down some of the lightsome discursive material of her frame into nuggets of English morality placed at the end of the story. The Bandellian tales of Boaistuau and Belleforest he likewise reproduces almost word for word, and subsequently demonstrates the fruits of this practice in his own translations from the original. In the story of the Lord of Virle, for instance,[12] which is narrated by Bandello in clear and lively style, Painter inserts classical references, sermons, letters, complicated erotic metaphors and doggerel. He omits Bandello's tricky Spoletine peddler; brings Zilia to a mawkish scene at Virle's sickbed; notes that Charles VII "miraculously" drove out the English in 1451, and

[10] Painter, XXXII; Boccaccio, I, 10.
[11] Painter, XXXIII; Boccaccio, II, 2.
[12] Painter, XCIII; Bandello III, 17.

disparages the French "according to the flatteringe and vaunting nature of that nation." Zilia herself he commends for her unromantic concentration upon housework. As for her stubborn chastity, Painter is hard put to it for once to deal with this virtue, which in Bandello's version simply runs counter to the normal expectations of courtly love. The English writer contents himself with obscuring her motives and berating her savagely when she succumbs.

In his version of "The Duchess of Malfi"[13] Painter goes to even greater lengths to apply French elegance and Puritan morality to Bandello's journalistic account. In the Italian tale the Duchess is pleasure-loving, practical and frank. It is not her fault that she cannot find a second husband of suitable age and rank; she does the best she can. Her proposal to Antonio is matter-of-fact. Hatred, cruel and unreasoning, pursues the pair; the death of the Duchess, her maid and her children is mysterious and unadorned.

Painter, on the other hand, is clearly setting forth a drama, the moral of which shows a remarkable agreement with the viewpoint of the villainous brothers: the Duchess has demeaned the noble blood of Aragon by wedding "almost the simplest person of all the trimmest gentlemen of Naples." The reader must take Painter's word for it that marriage is for her "a maske and coverture to hide hir follies and shamelesse lusts." Antonio, unexpectedly turned Platonist, wants to keep love "an unspotted image," but in vain. "Beholde," declaims the author, "the first acte of this tragedy." One by one the others unfold, obscured by rant, cluttered with letters, soliloquies, "cursses and desputes." The tale winds its way to three times the length of Bandello's before it is capped with a set of banal couplets. The Duchess's death-scene, however, is staged with vivid and moving detail. Abruptly, the author's sympathy shifts; the erstwhile "female wolf or lionesse" is now simply a helpless woman crying to her God.

Painter, apparently unaware of his frequent contradictions, doggedly moralizes every important action without regard to its relationship to the plot. Nevertheless, the tales which he adapts usually contain, in addition to gusty rhetoric and a moral which can rarely be made to

[13] Painter, LXXXIX; Bandello I, 26.

cover the events, some remarkably vivid and well-told scenes. The sub-merged realist in him delights in such minute details as the behavior of hungry lions "bristling up their heare" and "stretching forth their pawes,"[14] specifies exact ages, times and measurements in neatly clerical figures, and detaches himself at times from his own rhetoric in a semi-humorous aside. For the most part, however, he yields precedence to the demands of his French models who insist upon infusing an ideal into Bandello's world from without, just as Marguerite tried to spiritualize her *contes*. In this process, religious and courtly values often become hopelessly confused, while the action of the characters follow an un-related pattern. This method simply widens the gap between the real and the ideal, as Boaistuau's and Belleforest's *Histoires* demonstrate; in an effort to unify the retreating elements, the author tends to distort each one, bludgeoning the reader on one side with exaggerated horrors or lascivious details, and on the other with moral abstractions divorced from the experience itself.

Thus the Italian "novell" made its appearance in English already split in the French fashion. The defect suited the temper of Painter's time, and his borrowed riches brought enjoyment to uncounted readers who were no more disturbed by their anomalies than was he. Geoffrey Fenton, however, who brought out in 1567 thirteen *Tragical Discourses* (later called *Tragical Tales*) taken from Bandello, was less moderate than Painter; he not only adopted the style of Belleforest, his only direct source, but he deliberately heightened it. With remarkable verbosity he extended the tales to as much as five times their original length in Italian, adding moral harangues and many allusions, both classical and English. He also contributed gross metaphors in the erotic military terms derived from Aretino, fulsome discussions of marriage and a generous seasoning of fiercely anti-Catholic invective.[15] In fairness to Fenton, it must be admitted that he appears to have witnessed at first hand many of the abuses cited in his interpolations.

In spite of the fact that his prose is deliberately artificial and shows not

[14] Painter, XLI.
[15] Hook, pp. 27-28, 30-31.

only the influence of the *Pléiade* but of Guevara,[16] it achieves a certain paradoxical effectiveness. This has little to do with the fact that Fenton was "one of the founders of euphuism,"[17] preoccupied with careful antitheses, rhetorical questions and alliteration, and delighting in similes constructed about legendary birds and beasts; it stems from a personal vigor which refuses to be drowned in words. The style, like the man, is complex and exasperating; his tales and his character both reveal warring elements which almost—but not quite—cancel one another out.

Geoffrey Fenton, soldier, political schemer, chauvinistic Englishman and congenital spy, was a disillusioned and often cruel realist;[18] Fenton the militant Puritan bigot and writer of fiery "discourses" was, at least on paper, a self-righteous guardian of public morals. He wrote in order to gain political preferment, dedicating his volume to Lady Mary Sidney; when he became politically secure, he sermonized no more. He was much hated, and saw much in his world to hate.[19] Attracted by temperament to the violent world of Bandello and Belleforest, he sensationalized it further, drew up rhetorical barricades against its license and depravity, and transmitted it to his countrymen entire.

Upon superficial reading, the tales give the impression of unity, but this effect is theatrical, and covers a multitude of contradictions. The fact that in Fenton's imagination every story is played upon a stage is evident from numerous comments: "...I have here exposed unto you a miserable accident, happening in our time, which shall serve as a bloody scaffold or theatre, wherein are presented such as play no parts but immortal and furious tragedies."[20] His Don Diego, too, thinks in these terms, and sees "the discourse of the tragedy ready to present his last act with the death of his mistress...."[21] In general, says Fenton, every evil life may be used as a "fable and stage play to the posterity of a multitude."[22]

In accordance with this concept, he utilizes as much realism as he can

---

[16] Matteo Bandello, *Tragical Tales*, trans. Geoffrey Fenton, ed. Hugh Harris (New York, 1923), p. 35. [17] Ibid.
[18] Ibid., pp. 18, 20. [19] Ibid., pp. 22, 24.
[20] Ibid., p. 188 (Argument, Tale IV).
[21] Tale XIII, p. 555. [22] Ibid., p. 560.

support upon his unwieldy "scaffold." A good deal of this is astonishingly vivid; the description of the thunderstorm in the story of Perillo and Carmosina is almost scientific in its objectivity; the amorous Livio goes to his love in "shoes of felt," wearing "his perfumed shirt, spidered with curious branches... with his wrought coif powdered with divers drugs of delicate smell."[23] Anatomical details are drawn with lascivious care which, in the story of Pandora,[24] turns into Senecan horror in the descriptions of the woes inflicted upon that "infant male, unlawfully conceived, bedewed as yet with the wet suds of his wicked mother, sprawling and breathing with a little air of life." In Fenton's imagery, too, this realism often results in exceptional similes, such as the picture of the Milanese lover coming down from the chimney looking like "a red herring dried in the smoke against the beginning of next Lent."[25]

To counterbalance his lusty scenes, Fenton announces his purpose of explicating each one so that "the frail youth of our country...may see how sure they are to feel the heavy hand of God, who blesseth the good sort with a plentiful gift of His grace, and punisheth the wicked with sundry sorts of affliction."[26] Since the tales themselves demonstrate no such neat pattern of reward and retribution, but most often deal with the attenuated symptoms of courtly lovers or with sensational crimes and accidents, the Deity invoked by Fenton is actually forced into a vacuum; He manifests Himself neither within human events nor outside of them. The reader must take Fenton's word for it that He insists upon chastity, fidelity and filial obedience; smiles upon matrimony, generosity and magnificence, and frowns upon adultery, greed, dancing, "lust of the body," Italians, Frenchmen and the "Babylonian or diabolical sect of Rome." He seems to be forced at times to yield sovereignty to purely human love, which "hath power to bring to unity the minds that lived in separation" and "make indissoluble peace with the quarrels which seem immortal"—and yet even this seemingly benign force may turn out to be cruel, unfair or merely "pleasant poison...of our sensual appetite." Behind the scenes, blind Fortune, "always jealous of the ease of man" is continually "laying her ambush."[27]

[23] II. [24] III. [25] V.
[26] VII, p. 333. [27] IV, p. 190.

Fenton's world, in short, subsists in an atmosphere of the most agonizing insecurity, but his first story, that of Anselmo and Angelica, hides this secret behind a reassuring chain of events. Given three ideal characters, love brings forth generosity, which breeds gratitude, which in turn leads to sacrifice, which evokes pity—and finally gives rise to magnificence. Since Fenton's "discourses" are not forced to run counter to the action here, the reader gains the impression that the cosmos of the *Tragical Tales* is ruled by moral law. From this point on, however, Providence is considerably less dependable.

Livio and Camilla are rewarded for their chastity, fidelity and connubial love by sudden extinction upon their wedding night. So, too, are Perillo and Carmosina, no less innocent, but unfortunately vulnerable to lightning. In the story of Pandora, Fenton proclaims, "Here the adulterers may see how justly God punisheth their infidelity and breach of oaths towards their husbands," but it appears that in actuality this fiendish female, after her child-murder, puts on her best attire and goes off visiting her friends. The lustful Lady of Chabrye, after causing five horrible deaths, ends her days quietly as a respectable governess. On the other hand, Giulia of Gazuola, flower of chastity, is mercilessly raped and the Albanian Captain's faithful wife is butchered by her spouse in bed. Genivera la Blonde, after committing every possible offence against good manners, good sense, the tenets of courtly love and the canon of filial obedience, finally becomes the bride of Don Diego, paragon of lovers. (Fenton himself seems to be baffled here; dropping the complexities of love altogether, he seizes upon the secondary character Roderico and works the whole affair into a demonstration of the virtue of friendship.)

These basic anomalies, however, are so obscured by Fenton's overlay upon Belleforest that even the modern reader is likely to pass over them while following the ramifications of plot and style. Douglas, in his excellent introduction to the *Tragical Tales*, notes that this author "had in no small measure certain great artistic qualities" and expresses wonder at the fact that he has been "overlooked."[28] While it is true that he demonstrates exceptional vigor, verbal facility and realistic skill, and

[28] Bandello, pp. 33, 37.

imparts to his adaptations a strong flavor of pious morality, he has actually reduced Bandello's vivid Cinquecento to a series of puppet dramas. Reality has given way to artifice; a misapplied ideal renders it still more sterile; and the author's language, reflecting his strenuous efforts to reconcile the two, grows ever more prolix and ornate.

What seems to be a final stage in this process is exemplified in George Pettie's collection of twelve tales, published in 1576 under the title *A Petite Pallace of George Pettie His Pleasure*. The title and dedication to his "Gentlewomen Readers" were supplied by the friend "R.B." who ostensibly submitted the series to the printer on his own initiative.[29] Pettie himself was thus enabled to display a sophisticated *sprezzatura*—real or feigned—concerning these "tragical trifles" which he avowed were originally told to his friends as light after-dinner entertainment.[30] As a matter of fact, however, the fundamental novella convention of oral transmission which had been overburdened by Boaistuau and Belleforest, ignored by Painter, and transformed by Fenton into humorless rant is here finally suffocated under an avalanche of words.

Pettie has been called "the first complete euphuist,"[31] but more important for this study than the technicalities of his style are the factors which seem to be responsible for its excess. Pettie himself was a cultivated, amorous, witty and superficial young man; his English blood was warmed by a French strain, and he was far more European in temperament than the Clerk of Her Majesty's Ordnance or her sermonizing political spy. Instead of the Puritanical rift between flesh and spirit which distinguishes Fenton's tales, Pettie exhibits an ironic lightness and gaiety which would be Boccaccian had he not been set down to spin out his "trifles" in Elizabethan England. The fashion in his social set was an attitude of self-conscious Christian morality with Platonic overtones and a strong emphasis upon the sanctity of marriage; the practice was as liberally erotic as circumstances would allow. Pettie is amused by this paradox and uses his eleven classical tales and one medieval saint's life as convenient screens. Not only does he give them a contemporary

---

[29] George Pettie, *A Petite Pallace of Pettie His Pleasure*, ed. Herbert Hartman (London, New York, 1938), p. xii.
[30] Ibid., pp. xxxiv, xiv.   [31] Ibid., p. xxxiv.

atmosphere, but he half conceals beneath their private allegory a good deal of gossipy material relating to the lives of his friends.[32] The printer's admission that he has "gelded" them[33] gives a hint as to the author's original frankness; for all his eloquent preaching, Pettie is no Puritan.

His irony pervades the whole collection, but, like the paradoxes of Fenton, is almost completely hidden beneath an impressive verbal structure. His contemporary readers—even those uninitiated into his personal allusions—could enjoy in his pages elegant samples of amatory debates, exempla and apothegms[34] while indulging their taste for ornament and display—for Pettie catered to current styles and carried everything to extremes. His letter to "R.B." indicates that he was deliberately trying to use "new fashions" in words—and these he equates with fashions in "cutting of beards, in long-waisted doublets, in little short hose, in great caps, in low hats and almost in all things." This tone of easy superficiality springs from an attitude which is quite different from the lively experimental spirit characterizing so much of the thought and activity of his time; it bespeaks the fundamental decadence at the heart of Pettie's borrowed and bedizened tales.

In the first place, he relinquishes literary reality; because his interest in his sources is perfunctory, all of the action is rendered abstract and remote. The characters, likewise, are used to cover the identity of living persons or to convey abstract ideas, and possess no vitality of their own. This method could still be justified if (as in Spenser) the ideals behind the story façade were so firm in the author's mind that they could be brought to life through poetic imagination and made to communicate with the real world in the language of the senses. This process, however, would not suit Pettie's purpose even if he were capable of using it; behind his intricate and apparently solid structure of words, his viewpoint remains inconsistent and elusive.

In the story of Sinorix and Camma, for instance, the reader is led through harrowing details which culminate in the triumph of chastity— only to find out that the whole affair was hardly worth the effort:

"...And can the preservation of one simple womans Chastitie, counter-

---

[32] Pettie, p. xiii.   [33] Ibid., p. xvi.   [34] Ibid., pp. xxiii-xxvi.

vaile all these confusions? Had not the losse of her chastitie been lesse than of her lyfe? Yes, and of so many soules, which...are in daunger of damnation by their own desperate and sodayne death?"

Apparently this noble lady has been wrong about being so right—a conclusion which Pettie mitigates by the observation that women always tend to go to extremes.[35]

The tale of Minos and Pasiphaë also suffers from inconclusiveness. After pointing out the lady's sins in meticulous detail, the author indulges in what seems to be a confidential aside: "...In my fancy her husband deservede some blame; for no doubt his suspicion without cause, caused her in such sorte to transgresse marriage lawes"—but before the reader has a chance to consider the implications of this view, Pettie has submerged it in a full page of rhetoric on chastity.

Pigmalion [sic] and Alexius, too, reflect the author's chameleon temperament. The former, before the fortunate affair of the statue, gives voice to a tirade against women which is so eloquently constructed that Pettie feels obliged to offer a personal apology.[36] Alexius, on his way to sainthood, flees from the female sex, is finally persuaded to wed, and then declaims a rapturous paean which forms a pleasant ending to the tale. However, it appears that it is by no means ended, for Alexius is scheduled for another reversal; in a kind of postscript to the plot he turns toward heaven, having in the meantime lost all his eloquence.

Pettie's ironic and playful tone concerning the wisdom of "recanting" his own former vows and abjuring feminine society altogether is seen in his introductory letter to "R.B." to be closely connected with his attitude concerning Alexius. However, if this author ever toyed with the idea of becoming a celibate himself, he had lost it by the time he came to the end of the last story. Here the irony is turned sharply upon the ascetic ideal itself, or upon its hypocritical exponents in the pulpit, and subtly confused with fashionable neoplatonism. If the ladies listen to religious teaching, says the author, they will be told by "maister Parson" to "have no respect of persons, but to love an other man or him selfe" as much as their husbands.

---

[35] Pettie, p. 37.   [36] Pettie, p. 242.

Thus the ideals which this popular little book purports to set forth as a guide to gentlewomen are by no means as clear as they would seem to be. Since the tales have lost almost all connection with physical reality as well, the author attempts to infuse vitality by the only means available to him—a dazzling display of words. His diligent and ingenious balancing of phrase and clause, his florid experiments with the *schemata verborum* and the classical and medieval devices of ornamentation reflect a similar trend in the literature of other countries—France, Germany, Italy and Spain[37]—which likewise covers a dearth of literary substance. The fact that Pettie chose to use the old tale in this way, however, indicates that it was ready for his sumptuous winding-sheet.

Still, minor adaptations of stories in less ornate style, some rhymed and some in prose, continued to appear sporadically in England through the turn of the century, testifying to the continuing popularity of the Italian novella and the French style. Considered in terms of genuine literary treasure, all of these, like the collections of Painter, Fenton and Pettie, are frankly stage-money—coins negotiable only in the world of illusion. Still, amid the scattered works of the fourteen-odd English writers making use of the novella materials at this time, several are noteworthy. Arthur Brooke's *Romeus and Juliet*, in poulter's measure, adapted from the version of Boaistuau, served as a source for Shakespeare. George Whetstone, George Turberville, Richard Lynch and "T.A." also rendered some of the old stories in verse, usually in jogging pentameter couplets or fourteeners. To Barnabe Rich belongs the distinction of breaking away temporarily from the affected, moralizing style borrowed from the French; the tales in his *Farewell to the Militarie Profession* are straightforward and untrammelled by the usual artificialities.[38] "Kinde Kit of Kingstone" gives all his tales a realistic English framework in *Westward for Smelts*, and transforms the courtly old tale of Madonna Zilia and the Lord of Virle into a Devonshire fabliau.[39] Robert Smythe demonstrates what is probably the lowest ebb in the telling of "Strange, Lamentable and Tragical Histories Translated out of French," for he

[37] Pettie, pp. xxix–xxxii.
[38] Albert Baugh, ed., *A Literary History of England* (New York, 1948), p. 429.
[39] Pruvost, p. 99.

not only adds to the horrors recounted by Belleforest, but stumbles over his translation.[40]

The names of Wotton, Warner, Lodge, Fortescue and Grimstone round out the list, but their efforts simply bear further witness to the fact that the well-worn plots have found no real new life in the English tongue. Nowhere has there appeared a teller of tales who could transform the popular Italian realism into universal terms by infusing into it human dignity and spiritual power inherent in the action. The humor which springs spontaneously from a detached view of the human condition, the sense of wonder and compassion arising from a genuine tragic view—both of these have retreated before a barrage of words. In this ancient and much-loved form the breach between the real and the ideal now appears to be complete.

It is at this point that the vitality which always remains latent within certain stories finds its way spontaneously into a new form of expression. The dramatic imagination, seizing upon the basic human conflict of the plot, rekindles life and restores reality. If the dramatist possesses spiritual resources as well as poetic gifts, the result is a genuine transformation. Shakespeare, Fletcher, Webster, Massinger, Shirley, Heywood and Marston all used materials borrowed directly or indirectly from Painter's collection,[41] with various degrees of success.

The limitations imposed by the dramatic form and the freedom achieved by allowing the characters to speak and act for themselves instead of through a moralizing narrator constitute major improvements over the tales. In some cases the result is a genuine creative achievement. Webster's Duchess of Malfi bears little resemblance to Bandello's matter-of-fact young realist or Painter's lustful sinner; in spite of the inconsistencies of the dramatic plot, she emerges as a high-spirited woman whose passion, courage and dignity act as catalysts to the somber forces of evil which surround her. Shakespeare's *Romeo and Juliet* soars into realms unknown to Bandello, Boaistuau or Broke, for the poet of genius, who is neither moralist nor cynic, is concerned with a daring possibility—the power of the human spirit over hatred and even death itself. On the

[40] Ibid., pp. 79-83.
[41] Baugh, p. 413; Painter, p. xviii.

human level, this hope leads to certain defeat; but the tragic events disclose a new dimension in which innocence and love, allied mysteriously with the unseen realm made real through the humility of Friar Laurence, win their eternal victory over the world.

This poetic transformation is very different from the process of "idealization" which Pruvost, in his clear and comprehensive study, postulates as the chief tendency of the English translations and adaptations of Bandello. The addition of "sentimental, idealistic elements"[42] initiated by the French translators is actually no idealization at all, but the forcible application of an abstract system to realistic material. The result, as we have seen, is a highly artificial representation of life, compared with which even the crass Italian realism appears honest and vital.[43] Pruvost's conclusion that the fashion for Italian tales in English actually inhibited or delayed the development of the novel[44] bears witness to the fact that what we have been observing in this chapter is not a link in a chain of development, but a break—and the virtual end of the traditional novella form.

[42] Pruvost, pp. 128, 129.
[43] The tendency toward mawkish sentimentality which mars the French and English novella translations has a profound psychological relationship with the preference for tales of violence and horror. Jung notes in his *Symbols of Transformation* that "…sentimentality is sister to brutality and the two are never very far apart." Carl Gustav Jung, *Collected Works*, ed. H. Read, M. Fordham and G. Adler (New York, 1953), IX, 428.
[44] Pruvost, p. 329.

CHAPTER EIGHT

REGRESSION TO A UNIFIED WORLD: BASILE'S PENTAMERONE

The fascination with words for their own sake and the forced ingenuity of sound and arrangement which mark the work of Pettie and the English euphuists is exemplified in Italy by the musical extravagance of Marino. Among his devoted followers was one who, pushing the baroque style to its paradoxical extreme, found his way back from affectation to the vitality of childhood. Giambattista Basile, court poet, soldier and civil official, playwright and philologist, was a typical writer of the early Seicento, but one more witty and more intuitive than most. When he set about to tell a series of fifty tales to amuse his confrères in the *Accademia degli Oziosi,*[1] he paid half-serious, half-mocking tribute to Boccaccio. The ten story-tellers of his frame were no *lieta brigata,* but limping, slobbering hags; his language was not the graceful Tuscan in which he had proved his poetic gifts, but dialect; his choice of tales, drawn from the primitive Neapolitan folklore, was original and naive. The result, printed posthumously and without correction by the author, turned out to be the "finest Italian book of the baroque period."[2]

Although at first glance it may seem that Basile mined regions extending beyond the traditional territory of the novellieri, there is a fundamental relationship between his material and the sources utilized

[1] Giambattista Basile, *The Pentamerone,* trans. from the Italian of Benedetto Croce, ed. N. M. Penzer, I (New York, 1932), ix.
[2] Croce bases his judgment of the *Pentamerone* (also called the *Cunto de li Cunti*) on content and on Basile's masterly use of the "light baroque" style. Ibid., li.

by all of the great tellers of tales. The line between *novella* and *fiaba* is by no means stable or distinct. A number of Basile's stories would fit into a traditional collection,[3] and several other Italian novellieri, particularly Straparola, have included folk-tales in their offerings. However, these writers have attempted to give homogeneity to their works by minimizing or suppressing the realm of wonder,[4] whereas Basile actually enhances it—and balances the effect with extraordinary realism. The result, in his *Pentamerone*, is a cosmos bursting with life and miraculously unified.

All of the richest and most ancient collections of stories include tales of the supernatural, sometimes Christian or Christianized, but more often stemming back to remote pagan sources. Grimm's theory—that all European folklore is derived from an Indo-European source which is firmly rooted in primitive myth[5]—goes back to a past which contains within its depths far more than folklore *per se*. Basile's ogres and dragons do not subsist in a realm which is separate from medieval, Renaissance or Seicento reality; they constitute a timeless aspect of life which customarily disguises itself within the literary form most congenial to the temper of the time. Basile, searching for the ultimate in wit, discovered it in the naive; from the crudest of dialect he contrived the most sophisticated literary diction—a usage so fantastic and extreme that it mocks itself without ever losing its hold on concrete reality. In remaining true to the character of his own age, he transcended it—a feat rarely accomplished without the aid of genius. Basile, although Croce has called him "almost the Dante" of the Neapolitan dialect,[6] was not a writer of exceptional gifts—but he invoked no ordinary muse. The spirit which animates his *Cunto de li Cunti* is that of the common people, irrepressible, unpredictable and wise.

In the world shadowed forth by these tales the dichotomy between real and ideal does not exist; the reader follows the events on an integrated level of experience, although his mind may distinguish separate

[3] This point will be more fully developed below.
[4] Sercambi, Morlino and Cieco da Ferrara also made some use of this kind of material. Basile, xlviii.
[5] Ibid., II, 288 (Stith Thompson's addendum).
[6] Ibid., I, lxiv.

elements. The most dramatic change in the milieu is seen in the fluidity, changeability and indestructibility of matter, which undergoes continual metamorphoses without losing a whit of its familiar solidity. Thus the commonplace is always potentially wonderful, but the wonderful never becomes commonplace.[7] Human life, instead of remaining at the mercy of time, space and cruel circumstance, reveals a kinship with a vague but powerful transcendent order which favors the weak, the helpless and the despised. Fools,[8] stepdaughters,[9] poor brothers or younger sisters,[10] and abandoned children[11] usually turn out to be victorious in conflicts with the rivals or enemies which threaten them. Good and evil, on a pre-religious level, are thus clearly defined through the action of the tales and are further supported by means of reassuring proverbs. Courtesy, humility, modesty, generosity, truthfulness and gratitude characterize the good; with one or more of these weapons the weakest protagonist may prevail, for "he who does good may expect good"[12] and "innocence is a shield...on which every malicious sword is blunted or broken."[13] As for the wicked, the prognosis is equally clear: "He who spits in the face of heaven gets it back in his own face,"[14] and "he who lives evilly will never die well."[15]

In the realm of love there is little sensual dallying for its own sake; chastity is threatened more often by incest[16] than by personal temptation; marriage is a common goal which finally becomes an ideal state (often symbolized by royal rank), to be achieved by all deserving lovers after a long train of difficulties.

The simplicity of these familiar patterns requires no explanation; every tale, however, is topped off with a neat apothegm which does not necessarily fit, but which serves as a note of adult sophistication in the candid world of the child. Basile, whose subtitle "*Trattenemiento de' peccerille*" seems to be as ambiguous and mocking as the tone of his embellishments, never loses touch with the essential quality of his realm for

---

[7] "The concentration and tension of psychic forces have something about them that looks like magic." Carl Gustav Jung, *Collected Works*, ed. H. Read, M. Fordham and G. Adler, IX (New York, 1953), 219.

[8] I, 1; I, 4; III, 8; III, 5.   [9] III, 10; IV, 7.   [10] IV, 2; III, 4.
[11] III, 2; V, 8.   [12] III, 5, p. 251.   [13] V, 5, p. 129.
[14] Ibid.   [15] II, 9, p. 285.   [16] II, 6; III, 2.

all that. Here the reader may share the hypersensitivity of the child to sights, sounds, tastes and odors; his sense of weakness in a hostile and confusing world; his innocence of theoretical and even practical concepts; his fundamental need for consistency and order, and his spontaneous and imaginative exaggeration. By means of Basile's Rabelaisian fluency the reader is also made to experience something very like the dawning of verbal concepts, manifesting itself in repetition, rhyme, alliteration and the playful use of synonyms and catalogues.[17] And, since the author delights in filling the tales with countless references to children's games, the atmosphere is lively and free. Other aspects of the child's world are exemplified in the miraculous fulfilment of wishes, the use of sweetmeats as a standard for luxury or excellence[18] and an occasional demonstration of unabashed coprophilia.

More important than all of these, however, is the feeling of serene detachment which pervades this domain. As we have seen in preceding chapters, this is a quality which has become more and more difficult for the novellieri to maintain as the split between the rational and irrational sides of human nature has widened. In the *Pentamerone*, detachment is achieved without effort. Since it results from the consciousness of a supernatural order lying beyond the scope of human reason, its immediate effect is a liberating one, and its extra dividends are vitality and humor. Another effect, less easy to accept, is a seeming callousness to human suffering. An old woman may watch herself skinned alive (I,10), hands or ears may be sliced off without a qualm (III,2 and II,3), a stepmother may have her neck smashed under the lid of a chest (I,6) and a little talking fox with whom the heroine has spent an idyllic night in the woods can be murdered by her at a blow and drained of its blood (II,5) — all with matter-of-fact thoroughness and dispatch.

The scale of values which prevails here is primitive, but by no means as cruel as it seems. In the animistic child-world everything partakes of life; mutilation and death are consequently unreal—temporary at their very worst. They simply furnish appropriate means to foil those agents

[17] Although Basile uses these devices in a highly sophisticated manner, they paradoxically retain a childlike character.
[18] I, 7, p. 66; I, 10, p. 102; I, 4, p. 47.

which are working counter to the good, and leave effects no more permanent than those suffered in dreams.

There is, in fact, but a short distance between the partially sophisticated child-world of Basile, attached at countless points to the life of seventeenth-century Naples, and the mysterious territory of the unconscious. The path traverses the scholarly region of the folklorists, where a few signs point the way. Stith Thompson, quoting Axel Olrik's formulation, shows that folk-tales are usually concerned with the confrontation of opposing characters, with the main action limited to two persons at a time, and that the odds are in favor of the weaker, younger or least promising contestant. Simplicity of plot and character, repetition, and lack of variation in pattern are seen in all of these expressions of primitive culture.[19] These same characteristics, however, are also found in a completely wordless realm.

It is here that we move from literature to the hidden regions of the psyche, charted with extraordinary insight and erudition by Jung. The loss of the supernatural dimension in the modern world is to him a clear symptom of its spiritual malaise; he deplores even the semi-scientific expedient which he has devised to counteract it. "Only an unparalleled impoverishment of symbolism," he explains, "could enable us to rediscover the gods as psychic factors, that is, archetypes of the unconscious."[20] His system of "archetypes," then, is a classification of the fundamental psychic forces—hidden, but shared by all of humanity—which in earlier times were expressed in terms of myth, religion and folk-tale. The realm of the fairy story, peopled by "half-gods," stands midway between the worlds of myth and of reality; the relationship is fruitful and complex. "...The world of half-gods is anterior to the profane world and produces it out of itself, just as the world of half-gods must be thought of as proceeding from the world of gods."[21] The princes, talking bears and magic horses are projections of the unconscious; the battles, trials and blissful unions, as cryptic and as intense as dreams, are intimately related to the struggles of every human being to achieve

[19] Stith Thompson, *The Folk Tale* (New York, 1946), p. 456.
[20] Jung, IX, 23.
[21] "The Phenomenology of the Spirit in Fairytales," Ibid., p. 250.

wholeness and integration.[22] Wedding the princess is no mere childish fantasy, "for to the degree that the young swineherd gains possession of the patrician, feminine side of himself, he...lifts himself into the sphere of royalty, which means universal validity."[23]

This powerful substratum of meaning explains the haunting, nostalgic quality of the best folk-tales, and their perennial popularity, even with adults.[24] The child, abandoned by its parents or subjected to humiliation and persecution, is not only a familiar folk-tale character, but the personification of a psychic state.[25] So, too, are the other "archetypes" classified by Jung, all of which appear and reappear throughout the *Pentamerone*. The wise old man or woman (I,9; I,5), the ogre (I,1; I,5) and the beneficent fairy (I,3; I,8) are common examples, like the dragon (I,7), the wonder-working tree (I,6; I,10; V,9) the horse (III,7), and the serpent (II,5).

The animism which pervades Basile's world bears witness to the important part played by the subconscious in the development of the tales—and here lies the secret of their freshness and vitality. It is interesting to note that even when the author is humorously employing his most extravagant stylistic devices, as in his countless mock-classical references to a personified Sun, he actually supports the primitive atmosphere of the tale.

In like manner he enhances the continual transformations which occur throughout the stories by means of his own baroque taste for violent contrasts and contradictions. Under his hand the sudden changes from excrement to gold and jewels (I,1; V,1), maiden to bear and bear to maiden (II,6), serpent to prince (II,5), sickness to health (I,2), mutilation to wholeness (III,2), age to youth (I,10; IV,1) and death to life (I,7; II,5;

[22] "Being a spontaneous, naive and uncontrived product of the psyche, the fairytale cannot very well express anything except what the psyche actually is." Jung, IX, p. 239.
[23] Ibid., p. 251.
[24] This is attested by the Disney adaptations and the success of even the most debased form, the pseudo-magic of television commercials, in which doves and tornadoes transform kitchens, washing-machines grow like Jack's beanstalk and a White Knight, "stronger than dirt," gallops through the countryside, cleansing a soiled world with a flourish of his lance.
[25] Jung, IX, 180.

v,7) become a rhythmic movement from the most horrible reality to an ideal beyond the reach of poverty, pain and time.

It is in his extraordinary evocation of the real, however, that Basile most fully transcends his medium and perpetuates not only the tales themselves but the most intimate character of the Naples from which they sprang. It is impossible to read the *Pentamerone* without breathing the air of this ancient city, hearing its sounds and language, assuming its customs and absorbing that richly laden atmosphere. There Gagliuso's resourceful cat catches mullets from the Fish Rock (II,4); here Cienzo turns to bid farewell to the Piazza Larga, the Gelsi, the Loggia di Genova and all the places dear to him and to the heart of Basile (I,7). Here we find under our feet the treacherous cucumber peel, dropped by rogues to make us slip (III,7); we yawn with hunger and cross the yawn for fear of evil spirits; we learn that the best diet for madmen consists of a hundred eggs, that during childbirth it is salutary for the mother to blow into a vase, and that Lent is pleasant in Taranto. We watch the women smoothing their foreheads with glass balls and bleaching their long hair in the sunshine; we catch glimpses of chamber-pots, and spy on the vain girls busy with their pumpkin-water, rouge and curling-tongs; we sniff the appetizing odor of *piccatigli e ingratinati*, and hear afar off the sound of the bishop's bell, of children's shouts, of trumpet and *tarantara*.

Basile's love of the concrete, coupled with the Seicento habit of exaggeration and distortion, leads him very often into a kind of naturalism which seems to look forward to the century to come. The harshness of his view, however, is tempered with humor and equanimity. Beginning with the ten filthy old storytellers of the frame, each one distinguished by a loathsome adjective, he proceeds to weave into the ordinary description of the tales a series of pictures so repulsive that they seem to be mocking reality itself. Most noteworthy of these is the self-inflicted flaying of the crone in the tenth tale; a close second is the account of the three dysenteric nuptial nights endured by the princess Milla, mismated to the drunken German lord (III,5). Here the author revels in ironic euphemisms so rich in range and association that they all but transform the squalid details—until he chooses to banish the illusion in a final blast of fetor. Two more dreadful old women (I,10) along with Grannizia, *la quintessenza dei cancheri...con la testa pidocchiosa*, and the warty ogre in the same tale (III,10) show the human body as conglomerate deformity; the superglutton (II,10) reveals it in action. The wasting disease of the Princess of Campolargo (IV,2) and the scalding of Caradonia's daughter (III,10), like the skinning of the old woman, record its decomposition with shocking clinical detail.

Basile, however, is not satisfied to limit his use of reality to descriptions, allusions and grotesques; he finds means to insert sizable portions of it in the form of classified lists of ordinary things—fishing tackle (I,9), Neapolitan food (I,7), medicines (II,2) feminine finery (III,10), musical instruments (IV,2) and birds (IV,8). He also uses it ironically in his figures of speech, most of which are derived from the most commonplace activities. Nella, for instance, is gifted (in butchers' or in housewives' parlance) with the "prime cut of beauty" (II,2) and Prince Ciullone's royal aunt, helping him to gain access to his beloved, speaks like a tailor. "Then," says she, "when you have the cloth and the scissors in your hands it will be your own fault if you do not know how to make use of them," (II,3).

Another of Basile's characteristic uses of metaphor is his repeated combination of classical allusions with realistic terms in the vernacular. Cupid, for instance, is "that false blind boy, son of a cripple and a drab" (I,10) and Dawn points out to the birds the *macriata* which Aurora has daubed upon the sky (III,3).

In general, then, the author's use of realism can be seen to be a combination of the oral tradition (which he follows meticulously)[26] and a number of light-hearted literary devices of his own. At unexpected points he also inserts proverbs of a very bitter flavor, quite different from the complacent apothegms with which each *trattenimiento* begins, and from the naive optimism of the tales themselves: "The itch is bad, but a scab is worse" (IV,9). "Fine words and ill deeds deceive both fools and wise men" (II,4). "A prince's love is like bottled wine, good in the morning and bad by nightfall" (IV,2).

A final, paradoxical addition to the *Pentamerone* is the series of four satiric eclogues, one of which is placed at the end of each of the first

[26] Grimm's comment in *Kinder- und Hausmärchen*, quoted in Basile, I, lxix.

four days of story-telling. *La Coppella* mercilessly exposes the sordid truth disguised by wealth and fame; *La Tintura* reveals the moral ambiguity and corruption of Basile's actual world; *La Stufa* is an expression of weary satiety, and *La Volpara*, in the form of a satiric dialogue, excoriates avarice and greed. All of these are compounded from specific examples taken from contemporary life. Their function is similar to that of Boccaccio's plague—to set off the ideal realm of the tales from the appalling realities of human existence. Although the method of the poet here is the exact opposite of Des Périers' expedient of enclosing his set of realistic tales within dreamy lyrics, the purpose is fundamentally the same: to present both aspects of a divided world, and thus—as far as possible—to unify it.

Basile, however, has achieved a remarkable degree of integration within the tales themselves, and, like Chaucer and Boccaccio, he presents a world complete. This achievement is noteworthy, not only because he cannot be compared with them in literary stature, but because by his time the split between real and ideal had widened to a chasm. To bridge it he was forced to discover supernatural materials with solid attributes—and these, by a stroke of genius, he found in popular tradition. He was not the first to explore this field; Straparola, too, and a few others, had used such tales as part of a series of novelle, modifying them to fit the fashionable pattern and presenting them "often metamorphosed into bourgeois stories shorn as far as possible of the marvelous...."[27] Basile did just the opposite; he boldly seized upon the world of wonder which rested invisible in the Neapolitan folk-consciousness and brought it into the light, endowing it with living sounds, odors and colors, interweaving into its tenuous fabric a thousand strands of homely custom and familiar detail. The result is a real world—the domain of neither courtier, bourgeois nor peasant, nor yet a principality comprising these separate degrees; it is a spacious terrain in which rank is supremely mobile and symbolic. Considered from the point of view of the Boccaccian form, Basile's typical tale may be called the proto-novella.[28]

[27] Basile, I, xlviii.
[28] The folk-tale, of course, constitutes the raw material of many other forms as well, but we are concerned here with the development of a single one.

This relationship may be clearly traced within Basile's own collection, which is not completely homogeneous; some of the stories appear to have already lost some—or most—of their primitive characteristics, and could easily be classified as various types of novelle. The story of Cecio and Renza (III,3), for instance, is distinguished from the typical folk-tale by its tragic ending, as well as by its romantic tone and sentimentalized rhetoric. The tenth tale of the fourth day is simply an exemplum dealing with pride. The tales of Pinto Smalto (v,3) and Sapia (v,6), which are concerned with matrimonial trials, would fit (with some toning down of the magical element in the former) into any traditional collection. So, too, would the three tales which follow the fabliau pattern (II,10, III,4 and IV,4) and one which mingles fabliau elements with a more complicated plot (III,9). Sexual trickery, coarse behavior or a tone of disillusion sets off each of these from the purest type of folk-tale. The case of greedy Saporita (IV,4), in fact, shows an ironic reversal of values; she is rewarded with supernatural good fortune for tricking her husband, and lives in happy sloth and gluttony ever after.[29]

Among the finest and most typical stories of the *Pentamerone*, however, are ten or more which may be recognized as the original sources of such immortal favorites as "Puss in Boots" (II,4), "Cinderella" (I,6), "Rapunzel" (II,1), "Sleeping Beauty" (v,5) and "Hansel and Gretel" (v,8). Working from derivative or related sources, later writers presented these to the world's children in simpler form, with the changes of name and detail which always occur in adaptations arising from oral tradition. Basile's treasure-trove, meanwhile, remained locked in dialect. Felix Liebrecht's monumental German translation first broke the chains in 1846[30] and disclosed the fact that no one has ever told these stories better than Giambattista Basile. The riches which he gathered together and polished with such fantastic care have proved, so far, to be of interest chiefly to scholars and folklorists, but the fifty rare coins are no less valuable because of that. Their substance is fairy-gold—that elusive element which may at one moment appear as broken crockery or the droppings

[29] This tale is obviously a potential fabliau. When the supernatural begins to exhibit perversity, it is close to extinction.
[30] Basile, I, lxix.

of a goose, but which, in the hands of the simple-hearted, may purchase a kingdom.

Children may recognize and claim this demesne, but the author has by no means reserved its pleasures for *li peccerille*; he has brought it into audacious connection with the crassest realities of adulthood—mocking, satirizing, quipping, burlesquing at every step—without the slightest damage to the spirit of wonder which pervades the whole. And as he has, with wry magic, infused the world of childhood, of dreams and of hidden psychic forces with the particulars of his own age, so has he lifted up a portion of that Janus-faced Seicento into a universal realm where men may live with gusto, hoping and achieving impossibilities, trusting in the powers of good, and merrily bearing witness to the unending miracle of human life.

It is impossible to assess the full importance of the *Pentamerone* without some particular consideration of its style, which not only sets off the tales from their analogues, but constitutes a curious paradox. On the surface, its sophistication appears to be at odds with the simplicity of the material. A careful reading, however, reveals the fact that in one very important way, the expression *is* the tales.[31] In comparison with Basile's verbal jets, floods and fountains, the more familiar forms of these same stories, finding their way from related sources into French and German, are like quiet ponds. They are authentic, universal and charming, but they do not possess the life of *Lo Cunto de li Cunti*.

The baroque style itself defies all clear analysis and definition. From one point of view it is nothing but bad taste, extravagance and excess; from another, it expresses profound psychic disturbances, characteristic not only of the Seicento, but of the modern world. Wylie Sypher sees reflected in its perversities the failure of Renaissance optimism, and regards it as a sign of "anxiety and repression."[32] René Wellek, in compiling a symposium of opinions, shows that such writers as Gonzague de Reynold, Eugenio d'Ors, Paul Hankamer and Ludwig Pfandl read major

[31] This is apparent even in the English translations. A study of Croce's Italian version (which is, of course, closer to the original in phonetic values than any other translation) makes the fact more obvious.
[32] Wylie Sypher, *Four Stages of Renaissance Style* (Garden City, New York, 1955), pp. 102, 107, 114.

philosophical implications into the baroque, and that others, including Américo Castro and Leo Spitzer, attempt to "correlate stylistic and ideological criteria." Among the most interesting hypotheses for our purpose are those of d'Ors and Pfandl. The former detects in the baroque style an expression of "the naturalness of the supernatural"—a kind of "identification of nature and spirit." Pfandl, on the other hand, regards it as an expansion of the "supposedly innate Spanish dualism of realism and idealism" into an antithesis far less solid and serene—that of "naturalism and illusionism." Even more interesting with relation to Basile's fluid semantics is the view of Leo Spitzer, who believes that baroque artists are exceptionally "conscious of the 'distance between word and thing,'" and that they "'perceive the linkage between meaning and form at the same time as they see its falling-apart.'"[33]

To all of these writers, the style betrays some aspect of the crucial split between the rational and irrational sides of man's nature. Odette de Mourgues calls the baroque world-view "'a distortion of the universe through sensibility,'"[34] while De Sanctis sees in its stylistic excesses (exemplified by Marino) "a lyrical exaltation in words not felt by the soul" and the "corruption and dissolution of literature."[35]

The key-words which are used by these and other writers to describe the baroque—instability, insecurity, conflict, distortion, division, dissolution—all express a feeling of struggle to maintain identity; and this effort, on the whole, appears to offer little hope of success. Basile's verbal extravagances clearly reflect this struggle, but in the *Pentamerone* it is always a victorious and a fruitful one.[36] His constant merriment, however, and the clever satire and burlesque of his own affectations, are by no means a clear indication of his personal equilibrium. As Castro has pointed out, this kind of verbal "aggression" and "independence" is a

[33] René Wellek, *Concepts of Criticism*, ed. Stephen Nichols (New Haven and London, 1963), pp. 105-110.   [34] Ibid., p. 126.
[35] Francesco De Sanctis, *History of Italian Literature*, trans. Joan Redfern (New York, 1959), II, 703, 711.
[36] Like Crashaw, he effects a seemingly impossible union of Marinist style and spiritual vigor. In both cases this is brought about through the idealistic *quality* of the author's subject-matter and his identification with it. (The fact that Crashaw draws his vitality from the religious realm does not affect the basic comparison here.)

common enough reaction to a sense of insecurity.[37] So, too, may be the almost perverse extreme to which Basile carried out his enthusiasm for dialect—for by the end of his efforts he had not merely resurrected an old vernacular, but had concocted an artificial and macaronic form. His archaisms were not, like those of Spenser, calmly devised for musical and atmospheric effect; they were wrenched out in a kind of linguistic obsession which allowed no common Italian form to remain unchanged.[38]

As we move beyond the scope of vocabulary, we may see how Basile's poetic instincts and training led him to work this deliberately uncouth tongue into three distinct layers of decorations—the first two concerned with the sound and arrangement of words, and the third with their relation to reality.[39] These three patterns are also interwoven in a number of devious ways, and held together by the ubiquitous metaphor, which, in Basile's realm, becomes a basic law of nature.

The first kind of decoration comprises the basic devices of rhyme, repetition, alliteration, onomatopoeia and pun. In this highly poetic world, the atmosphere is surcharged with rhythm and echoing sound; anyone or anything may be caught up in its blind spell at any time. Rhyme begins with the simplest kind of nonsense chant—"*anola tránola, pizza fontánola*"[40]—and adds a magical note to dialogue:

> *Cuoco, cuoco della cucina*
> *Che fa il re con la saracina?*

It also serves to emphasize and round out proverbs:

> *La lingua no ha osso*
> *Ma può rompere il dosso.*

---

[37] Wellek, p. 108.

[38] Basile, I, lx.

[39] The figures and devices are somewhat obscured by translation into the Italian, but may be easily discerned nevertheless.

[40] Giovanni Battista Basile, *Il Pentamerone*, trans. Benedetto Croce (Bari, 1925), p. 281. (Italian version). The passage occurs in the third tale of the fifth day.

Onomatopoeia, in addition to its sensuous effect in legitimate words, provides for the *rucche-rucche* of doves and the proper sounds to use when talking to a bear.[41] Alliteration occurs everywhere—in old quotations like "*frito, freddo e fondo*" and "*solo, sollecito e secreto*," as well as extemporaneously, in such phrases as "*un mezzo miglio dalla marina*." Repetition is commonly used for dramatic effect in the details of the stories as well as in the dialogue. "*Beata te! Beata te!*" is a childish cry of jealousy,[42] while "*Buon dì, buon dì, Viola!*" forms part of the ritual give-and-take which provides the final joke in the story of Viola, the prince and the fleas.[43] As for puns, Basile playfully slips them in whenever he can: "*Strappato com'era del desirio, dava strappate al remo....*"[44]

All of these devices, primitive and spontaneous, depend primarily upon sound, whereas the next level moves fully into the realm of wit. Here everything depends upon rational arrangement. Beginning with Basile's fashionable anagrammatic play with his own name, "Gian Alesio Abbattutis"[45] and moving next into the realm of syntax, there are countless examples of the author's love of manipulation for its own sake. One of the best of these occurs in the story of "*Il Bianco Viso*," in which Renza's disillusioned series of antitheses occupies more than a full page.[46] The pleasure of balancing phrase and clause is also irresistible to Basile. In the story of "*La Vecchia Scorticata*," for instance, there is a typical display made up of three conditional clauses preceded by a trio of trumpeting apostrophes, all of which serve to announce the main clause, which advances majestically, trailing modifiers within modifiers, until it is brought to a halt by a semicolon; then come a pair of clauses decked out in flaming metaphor, ushering in a second sentence which carries in its train three adverbial phrases ranged side by side, each acting as escort for an objective clause bearing a traditional Petrarchan image—a golden cable, some burning coals, a transfixed heart.[47] Here the words alone,

[41] Basile (Italian version), II, 6, p. 233.
[42] I, 10, p. 133.   [43] II, 3, p. 204.
[44] V, 7, p. 315. (Although Croce scrupulously calls attention to the puns, they are often lost in translation.)
[45] Basile (English version), Vol. II, 170.
[46] Basile (Italian version), II, 3, pp. 36-38.
[47] Ibid., I, 10, pp. 132-3. (Sentence beginning "*O beccuccio di piccioncello mio...*")

almost without regard to meaning, form a disciplined, courtly procession; and since it is all a game, the effect is both humorous and cynical—the whole Seicento bound up in fifteen lines of convoluted prose.

Basile's most interesting devices, however, are those which reflect his shifting vision of reality—the simile, metaphor and hyperbole. The primary characteristic of all these, as he uses them, is their multiplicity; everything in the world of the *Pentamerone* is like something else, but the likeness is unstable; resemblances often follow one another in dizzy succession, seldom coming to rest in a permanent identity. The ogre is more hungry for human flesh than "the goldfinch for the nut, the bear for honey, the cat for fish, the lamb for salt or the donkey for brancakes."[48] Preziosa, hidden in the bearskin, is a candle in a "hairy lantern," a basketful of fine fruit hidden under leaves, a work of art in a prison of bristles, a treasure in a leather chest and a "show of all the graces."[49]

Metaphors may serve to exalt the commonplace or to bring ideas into relation with something more matter-of-fact, in the familiar style borrowed from Aretino.[50] Many are overworked conceits, like the mercantile images in a king's declaration of passion: "O inventory of the privileges of Love, by reason of which I am become a store of troubles, a warehouse of anguish and a custom-house of torment..."[51] The characteristic "diminishing metaphors"[52] appear everywhere, turning sad hearts into dishcloths and lending an air of humorous domesticity to descriptions constructed on a mock-heroic scale. This is especially noteworthy in the countless allusions to the Sun, who, in addition to controlling the diurnal rhythm of the *Pentamerone*, is kept busy with such duties as sweeping up shadows, administering golden pills to the sky and spreading sheets of pasteboard to catch the wax dropping from the

---

[48] Basile (English version), II, 2, p. 145.

[49] Ibid., II, 6, p. 175.

[50] Croce notes that Basile's "fan of conversation," for instance, is borrowed from Aretino's "fan of gossip." Ibid., III, 3, p. 245.

[51] Ibid., I, 10, p. 97.

[52] René Wellek and Austin Warren, *Theory of Literature*, 3rd ed. (New York, 1949), p. 198. Such metaphors are classified by the authors as typically baroque. Since the folk-tale itself expresses the same naive type of relationship in literal terms, Basile's metaphors often lend a curious effect, like that of double vision.

tapers of Night. Occasionally, "like a troublesome student," he is even evicted from his quarters. Night, too, has her own domestic routine, and may be seen spreading out her garments to prevent moths, while Aurora radiantly starts her day by emptying *"il pitare del vecchio suo, pieno di arenella rossa."*

Hyperbole, like metaphor, has multiple functions in this realm, idealizing the commonplace, exaggerating the repulsive or setting off implicit irony. A sleeping youth is "all lilies and roses"; an ogre's tusks grow down to his ankles; a lover weeps "pailfuls of sobs and buckets of tears," and the finger of a hag becomes the eighth wonder of the world.

Paradox, oxymoron and catachresis, described by Warren and Wellek as characteristic baroque figures, occur very seldom in the ornate prose of the *Pentamerone*.[53] Their absence, however, does not indicate that the classification is in error or that Basile's style does not epitomize the Seicento; it simply points up the fact that the contradictions and incongruities of the baroque view constitute the very essence of the material which he has chosen. The tales reveal a realm which invites verbal extravagance, but does not require it. In the end it transcends all fleeting decoration and absorbs it into something strangely solid and real.

It is Basile's baroque use of classical figures which displays his verbal ingenuity to the best advantage. Metaphors, similes and epithets appear in troops and battalions; antithesis begins to gibber; balance becomes fantastic; periphrasis runs wild. All of these serenely formal guardians of verbal etiquette join hands and begin to dance like maenads or children, following some occult wisdom more profound than that of reason. On the surface, this performance looks like a satire on the worst examples of mannerist or baroque style—crowds of depleted words struggling desperately to maintain control over a dissolving cosmos.

Actually, however, it is quite another thing. The difference lies in the *direction* of movement. One way leads downward, toward spiritual dissolution; its signposts are emptiness, artifice, incoherence, madness,

---

[53] These have been described as "expressions of a pluralist epistemology and a supernaturalist ontology." Wellek and Warren, p. 198. The philosophical analysis clarifies the reason why they are not useful in the fairy-tales, which require no verbal transformations of the cosmos. In the world of the *Pentamerone*, natural and supernatural are one.

death. The other is the way up, out of primordial chaos, and it is marked at first by confusion and multiplicity; out of these emerge concept, symbol, language, life. Basile has caught these opposing verbal tides just at the point where they appear to intersect, and has mingled them within the creative structure of his tales. The dwindling stream, guided into an ancient channel, begins miraculously to flow uphill.

A number of the outward characteristics of decadence bear a strong resemblance to those of childhood. Sensibility, weakness, extreme susceptibility to horror and beauty, egocentricity, cruelty, and preoccupation with words—these are only a few. It is not really surprising that Basile's deliberate distortions and proliferations accommodate themselves so promptly to the fairy-tale world. Here sounds, at first, are pleasurable for their own sake. As they are imitated and repeated, they fall naturally into rhythmic and alliterative patterns; rhyme and onomatopoeia become forms of play. As sounds become more complex and controlled they attach themselves experimentally to concepts, become symbols, combine, disappear and emerge reborn. Basile's long lists of objects and epithets reveal a highly sophisticated language sense; at the same time they reflect the child's "insatiable hunger for names" and "the sense of possession or domination of the object that knowing its name gives him."[54] Inchoate reality expresses itself continually in figures; everything exists by virtue of a likeness to something else.[55] The world gradually becomes filled with recognizable entities, all of which are alive and which take on reassuring domestic habits as they become more familiar. Quantities and qualities remain mysterious, and can be expressed only in hyperbole. Identity, whether of people or of things, emerges only after a disheartening struggle and innumerable transformations. Out of this dreamlike but intensely active effort, reality with its multiple names is slowly born. "The spirit apprehends itself and its

[54] Joseph Church, *Language and the Discovery of Reality* (New York, 1961), p. 74. Basile's words often appear to be clutching at a vanishing reality at the same time that they are creating it anew.
[55] "We metaphorize also what we love, what we want to linger over and contemplate, to see from every angle and under every lighting, mirrored in a specialized focus by all kinds of like things." Wellek and Warren, p. 197. (This is the process of enlarging and enriching the concept.)

antithesis to the 'objective' world only by bringing certain distinctions inherent in itself into its view of the phenomena and...injecting them into the phenomena."[56] In this process the child, like the primitive and the poet, is literally creating his world out of himself and what seems to him to lie outside of that self, using as his creative instrument the spoken word.[57]

It appears, then, that Basile, following some intuitive prompting, revitalized his language—perhaps unconsciously—by dipping it into ancient springs.[58] This half-artificial but strangely potent vernacular, in turn, brought his dreamlike tales into conjunction with the real world. The result, in the form of the *Pentamerone*, is an artistic achievement which has been recognized so far by only a few. Even if it had become more widely known in his own time, however, the book would have remained outside of the main stream of literature, for the Seicento was not attuned to the heart of a child.

Nevertheless, these fifty tales remain universal and unique. Two centuries after they appeared, the sundered world had become a source of even greater anguish to its poets than it was to Basile. Some of the most sensitive of these, following more sinister routes, were also to find their way to the strangely fruitful regions which lie hidden within the *Pentamerone*.

---

[56] Ernst Cassirer, *The Philosophy of Symbolic Forms*, trans. Ralph Manheim (New Haven, 1953), I, 178.

[57] "Language also reveals a noteworthy indifference toward the division of the world into two distinct spheres, into an 'outward' and an 'inward' reality; so much so, indeed, that this indifference seems inherent in its nature. Spiritual *content* and its sensuous expression are united....The two, content and expression, become what they are only in their inter-penetration...." Cassirer, I, 178.

[58] Wellek and Warren, in a brief and tentative discussion of the use of folk material in modern literature, note that "This might be called the view that literature needs constantly to renew itself by re-barbarization." Wellek and Warren, p. 236. Basile's accomplishment is distinctive in that he regressed to simplicity, satirized his own age and perpetuated it—all at the same time, and without any loss of quality.

CHAPTER NINE

CONCLUSIONS

The novella may be distinguished from related narrative forms by its well-traveled background and proclivity for appearing in groups. The novellieri were diligent collectors who brought out their wares in tens and hundreds in a tradition which, in the Western world, extends at least as far back as the thirteenth century. It is a tradition which satisfies the fundamental hunger for communication in several ways: it recreates familiar aspects of human life through the informal telling of the tales, reinforces their effect through discussion, and offers to the fictive audience a chance to participate as well as to receive. The illusion is that of easy conversation, which, even in cold print, tends to draw the reader into a convivial group.

The fact that most of the stories have been told and retold adds another dimension to this sense of community and imparts an indefinable richness to the flavor of the collection. The story-teller may simply transmit the traditional material in his own words or may impart to it a creative stamp of his own. His artistic credo is simple: he must entertain his hearers. If he is a skilful writer, he knows intuitively that his confidential style must mask a cool detachment which will enable him to deal with multiple and sometimes contradictory frames of reference as he moves from tale to tale. The varied nature of his resources almost automatically guarantees that he will not only provide amusing pictures of real life, but that he will also edify, with glimpses of the world of wonder, of mysterious or familiar supernatural forces, and the enactment of high ideals.

The human communication which is the very essence of the novella form depends upon this dual vision of the cosmos and its reconciliation in terms of life and action. No single tale need bear the whole burden, and none, in fact, ever does so. Each contributes to a totality which serves to relate all of mankind, with its manifold foibles, virtues and follies, within a universal framework of meaning. Human nature rarely fits a perfect pattern, but individual peccadillos cannot mar the whole. The security of this conviction, like that which permeates the world of Rabelais, finds its best and clearest expression in laughter.

In order to clarify this concept, we have surveyed the works of nine story-tellers, five of whom are also poets. Of the nine, all except Painter, Fenton and Pettie occupy first rank among the world's novellieri. It becomes clear, however, even to the casual reader, that they are not equally successful with the novella medium. With the passage of time, something seems to be continually escaping, like a vapor, from the groups of tales—sometimes from one side of the container and sometimes from the other. Within the space of three centuries the old stories become progressively less rich, less lively and less humorous—and since their authors are astute and skilful craftsmen, we may observe one after the other resorting to various expedients in an effort to restore the quality which seeps so mysteriously away.

This, as we have attempted to demonstrate, is the quality of wholeness, which depends upon a distribution and interpenetration of the real and the ideal, and reflects a balance between the rational and irrational sides of human nature. From what we have seen, the task of unifying these elements in a collection of traditional stories after the fourteenth century has become increasingly difficult. The results of the losing struggle are loss of detachment, humor and balance and a resulting impairment of style. Since it is only the extraordinary writer who can transcend the limitations of his age, we may attribute these difficulties to the changing times—the progressive cleavage and impoverishment of the human spirit through the exaltation of reason and the new science.

Boccaccio preserves an appearance of medieval dualism, subtly laughing it to scorn while he substitutes the purely human values of art and *cortesia*. The loss of the supernatural is still so novel in his tales that it constitutes a continuous witticism. If his world has suffered serious loss, he does not know it. Never does he lose his detachment; his communication with his selected audience is intimate and controlled.

The task is not so simple for Des Périers, whose environment and nature subject him to a serious conflict of the spirit; in his tales he is reduced to presenting a realistic half-world, whose very disillusion is enriched by implicit contrast with something hidden behind the scenes. Under these conditions, he maintains a remarkably effective and naive line of communication with his hearers, but betrays at times a tendency to manipulate words for their own sake.

His Queen, on the other hand, is more bold; she attempts to grasp the fleeting ideal by main force, and harness it to the reality of her world with rhetoric. In the attempt she loses her detachment as a story-teller, but retains it in her framework as a moderator of discussions. Humor in her tales disappears almost completely as declamations multiply; reality asserts itself with crudity and violence while the ideal, confined to words, remains stiff and lifeless. The essential rapport between speaker and listener—that mysterious *tertium quid* which transplants life directly from mind to mind—is gone.

The results of this kind of split are also to be seen in Fenton, while Pettie, abandoning reality and a consistent ideal, casually presents an effigy of life laden with an intricate embroidery of words. Bandello, however, communicates profusely and well on the level of the real. His cosmos may be incomplete, but he renders what he sees, without struggle or too much fashionable artifice. A competent photographer, he presents things by means of authentic detail, and includes sundry borrowed and outdated views for bulk and variety. The novella collection here has moved from its middle ground between the real and ideal and rests for a time in the realm of objective fact.

Physical reality, however, is by no means as stable as it appears to be. The human mind, baffled and wearied by too much of it—especially in verbal form—becomes insensitive. Any reporter knows that stories suffer by similarity or repetition; there must always be a new angle, a more sensational detail. Bandello's realism is not as faithful as it appears. He is a selective photographer; violence, lust and murder constitute the basis of his Cinquecento. Since he lacks artistic detachment, his is a sensationalized realism, turning false under his very hand. His communication as a novelliere, then, even on a single plane, is distinctly limited. Still, he remains one of the best of his time, in the age when tales proliferated like weeds.

If the basic task of the novella, like that of even the simplest popular forms, is to transmit a bit of life from speaker to hearer, it seems obvious that this function, through no fault of the novellieri themselves, has been progressively impeded since the time of Chaucer and Boccaccio. In the Cinquecento and even into the following century the well-worn stories are still circulating, along with more recent imitations, but they carry little vitality with them. It is no accident that the greatest story-tellers of the world have all been poets, who, like primitives, mystics and children, have the power of viewing man's dual world as one. In a cosmos bereft of correspondences, however, the old tales slowly lose their genuine idealism by a process which baffles the narrators themselves; the supernatural cannot be recreated for an audience which no longer possesses the means to receive it. Stories of human activity are leveled to the plane of the lusts and passions—the starkly physical world of cause and effect.[1] Eventually that world itself, cut off from meaning, becomes unreal.

It is this situation which prompted Basile to plunge into a medium which allowed him to extend false reality one step further—to grotesquerie and naturalism. In doing this he suddenly resurrected the missing half of the scale. The totality of consciousness which he rediscovered, however, was a primitive one. The novella as we know it could not be reborn from this nucleus because its identity as a form depends upon an extensive body of shifting but familiar content; it survives by means of repetition and tradition. By its very nature it can remain alive only if the audience to which it is presented responds to its range of values and continually reinforces them.[2]

---

[1] This aspect of reality in Chaucer, for instance, represents only the lower extreme of a continuum extending from earth to heaven.

[2] The stories of the Bible, too, although they subsist in a supra-literary structure, have undergone a comparable deterioration in the modern age, since for the majority they no longer

In the world of the novella, human beings appear as types, but they are no less human for all that; they form part of a meaningful and repetitive pattern of life, drawn from the whole collection and embodying the results of human experience. When Cervantes boldly set out to write the first *novelas* in Castilian, and, in the process, to ignore all of the traditional material which was available to him, he not only made a radical change in the pattern, but created characters who stand out as individuals. Some, like the boy thieves Rinconete and Cortadillo are drawn with stunning verisimilitude; others, such as the gypsy Preciosa are figures of romance; while in the *Coloquio de los perros* the two fantastic animals are nevertheless real dogs. Thus, although his *Novelas Ejemplares* are almost contemporaneous with the *Pentamerone*, Cervantes moves in a literary direction which is diametrically opposed to that taken by Basile. The Neapolitan's plunge into folklore takes him down to the hidden roots of the old novella; the Spaniard plants seeds which, in time, are to bring forth the dual aspects of a new genre.

El licendiado Vidriera, for instance, is both a psychological study and a disillusioned commentary on the external world. The reader easily identifies himself with this wise madman—but never completely. The process of dissociation which is evident in the Seicento must have still more centuries in which to work before a completely new kind of character can come into view. When this lonely individual finally emerges, confused and questioning, he becomes his own painful center of focus; from him the reader may gain new insight into the nature of reality.

The appearance of the short story in the nineteenth century shows this radical change of perspective, along with a rediscovery of the world of the unseen. Hawthorne finds the supernatural in the Puritan pre-

communicate truth in spirit or fact. Sporadic adaptations in the form of children's books and cinematic spectacles reveal incalculable losses of vigor and meaning. An example of successful "re-barbarization" of a series of Bible stories, however, is Marc Connelly's play "Green Pastures," which effectively restores the supernatural element by visualizing it through the primitive imagination of the Southern Negro. This also demonstrates the preservation of quality through escape into drama—but in this case it is only partial and temporary. A play, too, retains its life only if it continues to communicate in universal terms with its audience.

occupation with guilt; Poe dichotomizes himself into reason and feeling, but in his imaginative tales he creates vivid objective reality mirroring the states of his own sick soul. Conrad, on the other hand, begins his explorations in the natural world, which reveals sinister jungles and abysses corresponding to depths within the human psyche. The unifying symbol which was sought by the French *Symbolistes* with all the intensity of the saint and all the abandon of the damned,[3] becomes the keynote of modern literature, uniting subject and object at last, but on a lonely precultural level. The realm of the novella, which so clearly reveals the old ideals slowly losing their power, suffering displacement and turning into empty words, is gone beyond recall. In its place there is a cosmos strangely shifting and sinister. The nightmare frustrations and meta-morphoses of Kafka, the living death of Beckett's cold vision, speak now for a generation caught in the grip of an increasingly materialistic and lethal society.

Ironically, the search for the ideal realm of unity, beauty and peace is now entrusted by many to the practical powers of science. The use of hallucinogenic drugs as a means of restoring a total vision of the universe is as ancient as it is modern; never before, however, has it threatened to usurp the domain of mystic and poet. The portals which swing wide at the command of a minute quantity of chemical matter absorbed into a human body open unpredictably into Milton's Chaos, Dante's Inferno or the pellucid realms of the "Pearl" poet and St. John the Divine, but they are private spheres; there is no guarantee that the rash voyager, once embarked, will ever return.

The old tales exemplify a humble literary form, marked by *joie de vivre* and hampered by few pretences. They were never told in an effort to transform the world—but even they conceal a force more potent than any chemical formula. First, the novellieri, sustaining the tradition of communal song and story, strengthened the bonds of common humanity. Frankly disillusioned on one hand, they dispelled hypocrisy

[3] Wellek and Warren call attention to Emile Caillet's "remarkably unblushing and uncritical acceptance of equivalence between the pre-logical mind of primitive peoples and the aims of the *Symboliste* poets." René Wellek and Austin Warren, *Theory of Literature*, 3rd ed. (New York, 1949), p. 303 (note).

concerning the earthy side of man's nature; in equal sincerity they provided the means to render this vision comic—persuasive examples of another side, united with the first, but capable, under certain conditions, of gloriously subduing it.

Such tales bear witness to the transforming power of something within and beyond the human spirit; all of them remain triumphantly independent of language, custom and time. A citizen of the modern world may still, like Don Federigo, discover his greatest treasure by sacrificing it, or distil from a scene of violence and bestiality a lasting vision of beauty, like Giulia da Gazuola. In a sick age he may still, like Des Périers' gloomy patient, shift his gaze from himself to another living creature and suddenly find himself healed through laughter. Sounding the mysteries of Basile's living landscape, he too may vanquish his monsters unafraid—or, if a cruel stroke has made him mute, he may still, like the "litel clergeon," find miraculous means to sing. The finest of the old tales still emit a radiance whose source man seeks more earnestly than ever, in a darkening world, to rediscover within himself.

"...Man's natural condition is darkness...unless he turns towards a light which falls from a place beyond the sky. Humanism was not wrong in thinking that truth, beauty, liberty and equality are of infinite value, but in thinking that man can get them for himself without grace."[4]

[4] Simone Weil, "The Romanesque Renaissance" in *Selected Essays, 1934-1943*, ed., trans. Richard Rees (London, New York, 1962), p. 53.

LIST OF WORKS CONSULTED

Baldwin, Ralph. *The Unity of the Canterbury Tales.* Copenhagen, 1955.

Bandello, Matteo. *The French Bandello, a Selection: the original text of four of Belleforest's Histoires Tragiques*, ed. Frank S. Hook. Columbia Missouri, 1948.

— *Tragical Tales*, trans. Geoffrey Fenton, ed. Hugh Harris. New York, 1923.

— *Twelve Stories*, trans., ed. Percy Pinkerton. London, 1895.

— *Tutte le opere*, a cura di Francesco Flora. 2 vols. Italy, 1952.

Basile, Giovanni Battista. *Il Pentamerone, ossia, la fiaba delle fiabe*, trans., ed. Benedetto Croce. 2 vols. Bari, 1925.

— *The Pentamerone*, trans., ed. Benedetto Croce, N. M. Penzer. New York, 1932.

Baugh, Albert C. *A Literary History of England.* New York, 1948.

Boccaccio, Giovanni. *Il Decamerone*, a cura di Mario Marti. Milan, 1958.

— *The Decameron*, trans. Richard Aldington. Garden City, N.Y., 1930.

Bryan, W. F. and G. Dempster, eds. *Sources and Analogues of Chaucer's Canterbury Tales.* New York, 1958.

Burckhardt, Jacob. *The Civilization of the Renaissance in Italy*, trans. S. Middlemore. New York and London, 1929.

Cassirer, Ernst. *The Philosophy of Symbolic Forms*, trans. Ralph Manheim. 3 vols. New Haven, 1953.

Castex, P. and P. Surer. *Manuel des Etudes Littéraires Françaises*, II: XVIe Siècle. Paris, 1946.

Castiglione, Baldassare. *Il Libro del Cortegiano*, a cura di Carlo Cordié. Milan, Naples, n.d.

— *The Book of the Courtier*, trans. Sir Thomas Hoby, ed. Drayton Henderson. London, New York, 1928.

Chaucer, Geoffrey. *Poetical Works*, ed. F. N. Robinson. Cambridge, Mass., 1933.

Chenevière, Adolphe. *Bonaventure des Periers, sa vie, ses poésies.* Paris, 1886.

Church, Joseph. *Language and the Discovery of Reality.* New York, 1961.

Cross, Wilbur. *The Development of the English Novel.* New York, 1899.

Cummings, Hubertis. *The Indebtedness of Chaucer's Works to the Italian Works of Boccaccio.* Menasha, Wisconsin, 1916.

De Sanctis, Francesco. *Histroy of Italian Literature*, trans. Joan Redfern. 2 vols. New York, 1959.

Des Périers, Bonaventure. *Le Cymbalum Mundi précédé des Nouvelles Récréations et Joyeux Devis*, ed. P. L. Jacob. Paris, 1858.

Edel, Leon. *The Psychological Novel*. New York, 1959.

Frank, Joseph. *The Widening Gyre*. New Brunswick, N.J., 1957.

Frye, Northrop. *Anatomy of Criticism: Four Essays*. Princeton, 1957.

Griffith, Gwynfor. *Bandello's Fiction*. Oxford, 1955.

Hassell, James. W., Jr. *Sources and Analogues of the Nouvelles Récréations et Joyeux Devis*. Chapel Hill, N.C., 1957.

Holzknecht, Karl, ed. *Sixteenth Century English Prose*. New York, 1954.

Huxley, Aldous. *The Doors of Perception and Heaven and Hell*. New York, 1963.

Jourda, Pierre. *Marguerite d'Angoulême, Reine de Navarre*. Paris, 1930.

Jugé, Clément. *Jacques Peletier du Mans (1517-1582)*. Paris, 1907.

Jung, Carl Gustav. *Collected Works*, ed. Herbert Reed, Michael Fordham, Gerhard Adler. 17 vols. New York, 1953.

Jusserand, J. J. *The English Novel in the Time of Shakespeare*, trans. Elizabeth Lee. London, 1903.

Krapp, George Philip. *The Rise of English Literary Prose*. New York, 1915.

Krutch, Joseph Wood. *Five Masters: a Study in the Mutations of the Novel*. New York, 1930.

— *The Modern Temper*. New York, 1956.

Lee, A. C. *The Decameron: Its Sources and Analogues*. London, 1909.

Lefranc, Abel. *Grands Ecrivains de la Renaissance*. Paris, 1914.

Lewis, M. M. *How Children Learn to Speak*. London, 1957.

McManus, Francis. *Boccaccio*. New York, 1947.

Malone, Kemp. *Chapters on Chaucer*. Baltimore, 1951.

Mish, Charles, ed. *Short Fiction of the 17th Century*. New York, 1963.

More, Sir Thomas. *Utopia*, trans. Ralph Robynson. New York, 1935.

Navarre, Marguerite de. *L'Heptaméron*, ed. Michel François. Paris, 1960.

— *The Heptameron*, trans. Walter Kelly. London, n.d.

— *Les Marguerites de la Marguerite des Princesses*, ed. Felix Frank. Paris, 1873.

Owen, Charles, ed. *Discussions of the Canterbury Tales*. Boston, 1961.

Painter, William. *The Palace of Pleasure*. 4 vols. London, 1929.

Pettie, George. *A Petite Pallace of Pettie His Pleasure*, ed. Herbert Hartman. London, New York, 1938.

Piddington, Ralph. *The Psychology of Laughter*. New York, 1963.

Praz, Mario. *The Flaming Heart*. New York, 1958.

Pruvost, René. *Matteo Bandello and Elizabethan Fiction*. Paris, 1937.

Putnam, Samuel. *Marguerite of Navarre*. New York, 1935.

Raleigh, Sir Walter. *The English Novel*. London, 1894.

Richards, Ivor A. *Principles of Literary Criticism*. 4th ed. New York, 1930.

Rollins, H. and H. Baker, eds. *The Renaissance in England*. Boston, 1954.

Russell, David. *Children's Thinking*. Boston, New York, 1956.

Schoeck, R. and J. Taylor, eds. *Chaucer Criticism*. Notre Dame, Indiana, 1960.

Senior, John. *The Way Down and Out: The Occult in Symbolist Literature*. Ithaca, N.Y., 1959.

Shumaker, Wayne. *The Irrational in Literature*. Englewood Cliffs, N.J., 1960.

Sorieri, Louis. *Boccaccio's Story of Tito e Gisippo in European Literature*. New York, 1937.

Spingarn, J. E. *A History of Literary Criticism in the Renaissance*. New York, 1924.

Swan, Charles, trans. and W. Cooper, ed. *Gesta Romanorum*. New York, 1959.

Symonds, John A. *The Renaissance in Italy.* 2 vols. New York, 1887.

Symons, Arthur. *The Symbolist Movement in Literature.* New York, 1958.

Sypher, Wylie, ed. *Comedy.* Garden City, N.Y., 1956.

— *Four Stages of Renaissance Style.* Garden City, N.Y., 1955.

Taylor, Harry Osborn. *Thought and Expression in the Sixteenth Century.* 2nd ed. 2 vols. New York, 1930.

Thompson, Stith. *The Folk Tale.* New York, 1946.

— *Motif-Index of Folk Literature.* 6 vols. Bloomington, Indiana, 1955-58.

Tilley, Arthur. *The Literature of the French Renaissance.* 2 vols. New York, 1959.

Underhill, Evelyn. *Mysticism, a Study in the Nature and Development of Man's Spiritual Consciousness.* London, 1911.

Valency, Maurice. *In Praise of Love.* New York, 1961.

— and Harry Levtow, eds. *The Palace of Pleasure.* New York, 1960.

Wellek, René. "The Concept of Baroque in Literary Scholarship," *Journal of Aesthetics,* v (1946), 78-96.

— *Concepts of Criticism,* ed. Stephen Nichols, Jr. New Haven, 1963.

— and Austin Warren. *Theory of Literature.* 3rd ed. New York, 1956.

Weil, Simone. *Selected Essays, 1934-1943,* ed., trans. Richard Rees. London, New York, 1962.

Willey, Basil. *The Seventeenth Century Background.* Garden City, N.Y., 1934.

REPRINTS FROM OUR COMPARATIVE LITERATURE STUDIES

Through the University of North Carolina Press
Chapel Hill, North Carolina 27514

2. Werner P. Friederich. DANTE'S FAME ABROAD, 1350-1850. The Influence of Dante Alighieri on the Poets and Scholars of Spain, France, England, Germany, Switzerland and the United States. Rome, 1950 and 1966. Pp. 584. Paper, $ 10.00.

10. Charles E. Passage. DOSTOEVSKI THE ADAPTER. A Study in Dostoevski's Use of the Tales of Hoffmann. 1954. Reprinted 1963. Pp. x, 205. Paper, $ 3.50. Cloth, $ 4.50.

11. Werner P. Friederich and David H. Malone. OUTLINE OF COMPARATIVE LITERATURE. From Dante Alighieri to Eugene O'Neill. 1954. Fourth Printing, 1967. Pp. 460. Paper, $ 6.00.

Through Russell and Russell, Inc.
Publishers, 122 East 42 Street
New York, N. Y. 10010

1. Fernand Baldensperger and Werner P. Friederich. BIBLIOGRAPHY OF COMPARATIVE LITERATURE. 1950. Pp. 729. Cloth, $ 15.00.

6, 7, 9, 14, 16, 18, 21, 25 and 27. W. P. Friederich and H. Frenz (eds): YEARBOOKS OF COMPARATIVE AND GENERAL LITERATURE. Vols. I (1952) to IX (1960). Cloth, $ 6.50 per volume.

Through Johnson Reprint Corporation
111 Fifth Avenue
New York, N. Y. 10003

3. R. C. Simonini, Jr. ITALIAN SCHOLARSHIP IN RENAISSANCE ENGLAND. Cloth, $ 12.50.

4. GOETHE'S SORROWS OF YOUNG WERTER, TRANSLATED BY GEORGE TICKNOR. Edited with Introduction and Critical Analysis by Frank G. Ryder. Cloth, $ 8.00.

5. Helmut A. Hatzfeld. A CRITICAL BIBLIOGRAPHY OF THE NEW STYLISTICS APPLIED TO THE ROMANCE LITERATURES, 1900-1952. Cloth, $ 12.00.

13. Horst Frenz and G. L. Anderson, eds. INDIANA UNIVERSITY CONFERENCE ON ORIENTAL-WESTERN LITERARY RELATIONS. Cloth, $ 15.00.

15. Dorothy B. Schlegel. SHAFTESBURY AND THE FRENCH DEISTS. Cloth, $ 12.50.

19. P. A. Shelley, A. O. Lewis Jr. and W. W. Betts Jr., eds. ANGLO-GERMAN AND AMERICAN-GERMAN CROSSCURRENTS, Volume One. Cloth, $ 15.00.